SO-AYW-649

Step-by-Step
Basketball
Fundamentals
for the Player and Coach

by John W. Scott

Photography by Glen Ricks

© Copyright 1985 J. W. Scott
All rights reserved.
ISBN: 0-934126-71-2

This book or any part thereof may not be
reproduced in any form whatsoever, whether by
graphic, visual, electronic, filming, microfilming,
tape recording, or any other means, without the
prior written permission of Randall Book Co.,
except in the case of brief passages embodied
in critical reviews and articles.

First Printing, May 1985
Printed in the United States of America

Randall Book Co.
Salt Lake City, Utah

"A VERY SPECIAL AGONY"

It starts as a dream in a little boy's mind, the fame, the glitter, the pride. It's all a hope, a prayer, a quest; a sleeper's reality.

The trial is hard and long; the vehicle—yourself; the fuel—desire. Time passes slow, yet too quickly. You don't reach all your goals and it seems that with more time you would, but that's part of this grueling process.

You are disappointed often, and at first success is slow and almost seems forever in coming, but that sparkle, that desire within, that belief in yourself and that disbelief of others in you keep you going, striving, pushing, and straining every fiber of your body.

Many obstacles stand in the way. Each seems bigger than the last, but you still go on. Sometimes you feel nothing can stop you, and other times you feel you'll never make it. As time passes on, these trials become stepping stones on the stairway to your goal.

Time, pain, failure, sweat and more pain. Work, desire, hustle, success, and more sweat. You fall, get up, and fall again. You stand, you trip, you rise again.

Why? It's simple. Because it's all part of the struggle to be the best, part of the trial you must endure. It is all part of something only you can understand,

It's a very special agony.
John W. Scott

DEDICATION

To God and my family who brought me into this world and brought me up in it. Dad, Mamma, Granddaddy Scott, Susan, Roy, Eric, Sherri, Marty, and all my family, to you my wish is that I will always make you proud and live my life as you have taught me. Without your belief and support I would never have had the courage to try.

To all my friends and those few coaches of past and present that have encouraged, loved, supported me, and helped me to learn to respect myself. To Lori.

A special thanks to my Norwegian grandpa and grandma who toiled for twenty years to reach their dream of coming to America so that one day I, too, could have the freedom to live mine. . . .

CONTENTS

INTRODUCTION

The purpose of this book is to make available drills, information, and ideas to players who have the desire to develop and improve their skills.

Having played at the high school, college and professional levels, and being a dedicated fan and basketball coach now, I have read all the books I could find on basketball. But nowhere have I ever found a book that simply and completely explains many skill areas and demonstrates drills for developing all of them. A book that helps a player to teach himself the various fundamental skills of the game as well as the more advanced.

This book includes chapters on shooting, dribbling, ball-handling, passing, defense, the "triple-threat" as an offensive tool, rebounding, cutting and others. There are sections at the end of each chapter for coaches which explain how to implement the drills in each chapter into a team-oriented practice. Throughout the book are new ideas and concepts.

No matter at what age or level of basketball you are, if you want to develop your game, this book can help you become a better basketball player and coach.

John W. Scott

THE "ART" OF SHOOTING

Shooting's a game of confidence.

Larry Bird

—N.B.A. Rookie of the Year 1979-80
—World Champion Boston Celtics
1981; 1984
—M.V.P. in NBA 1984-1985
—N.B.A. All Star Team

I wasn't a natural shooter and it was something I had to work on.

Julius Erving—"Dr. J."

—M.V.P. in N.B.A. 1981
—N.B.A. All Star Team
—World Champion Philadelphia '76ers
1981

Work on your shooting so you're as dangerous as possible . . . You've got to know when to shoot and where to shoot . . . Take your shot when you are open—but be sure the shot you take is a good one for you. Whether it is a good shot to take depends on a player's range and accuracy. . . .

Jerry West—"Mr. Clutch"

—N.B.A. Scoring Champion 1970
—N.B.A. All-Star Team
—World Champion Los Angeles Lakers
1982
—Member of Basketball Hall of Fame

1

THE "ART" OF SHOOTING

In this chapter you can learn:

- •The most important basketball skill—shooting!
- •How to develop confidence in your shooting skills.
- •Your ability to shoot is in direct proportion to your practice habits.
  - —Nine shooting drills that will give shooting mastery
  - —Workout schedules for shooting from every offensive position
  - —Shooting drills for team practice

It is not my intention in this chapter to explain "how" to shoot a basketball. Anyone reading this book should have some of these fundamental skills. Instead, I want to stress the importance of practicing shooting on a consistent schedule and to introduce drills for shooting.

Shooting is the most important skill to master in basketball because, "Basketball is all about putting the ball in the basket." Anything that you practice on an individual or team basis is oriented to score points. Many of the skills of basketball such as rebounding, defense, passing and cutting are what I call

"HABIT SKILLS." Once you have mastered these fundamental skills of the game, you have no need to practice them on a regular basis. "Habit Skills," once mastered, are committed to memory, just as eating or writing. They become "second nature," only requiring use of your memory to tell your body when to perform the necessary skill. That is why before basketball games at every level you do not see players go out and spend time warming up by practicing rebounding, passing, or defense. They practice shooting! Confidence in performing "Habit Skills" comes from a knowledge of how to perform them correctly.

Confidence, success and consistency in shooting a basketball can only come from practice on a regular daily basis. Shooting is an art. To shoot a basketball well requires use of your memory, confidence, the motor skills of your body (arm, elbow, wrist) and a basketball. You can learn how to shoot a basketball correctly. But to shoot in a game when under pressure with confidence and accuracy, this is an "art," and must be practiced regularly and consistently to be successful.

Concert pianists practice hours every day. Singers, entertainers, artists and professionals of all kinds have all developed skills. They never forget how to use them but, if they do not practice, they will not perform well; they are not as sharp. Let us define the words "skill" and "art."

Skill—How to do a specific task correctly.

Art—The ability to perform with confidence, consistency, smoothness and success.

Millions of people know how to play a piano but cannot perform in front of a large audience. They have knowledge, but they are not proficient in the "art" of playing the piano. Millions of people know how to sing. We all have sung—Birthday parties, Christmas carols, at church or with a school choir, etc.—we all know how to sing. But how many of you are willing to sing a solo? If you had practiced a song five times a week for two months would you be more willing to sing a solo? Yes, you would. To the skill and knowledge you had, you have added art and confidence in performing.

This principle applies to shooting a basketball. How many basketball players in a game do you see hesitate to take a shot

5

from 17 or 20 feet away from the basket? How many hesitate to take a last second game-winning shot? They know how to shoot. They have made those shots in practice, so why do they hesitate? The answer is simple, they have not developed the "art" of shooting a basketball. Developing the art of shooting in game situations comes from consistent daily practice. There is a principle which states:

"Practice leads to confidence
Confidence leads to success,
Success leads to more confidence. . . ."

The more of anything you do in life, the more confidence you have in doing it. If you are confident when performing whether playing piano, singing or shooting a basketball, you will be successful at doing it. Consistent practice on a regular daily basis is vital in developing your ability to be an "artist" at shooting the basketball.

Now that you understand the importance of regular prectice, you need to define what and how you will practice. The drills you practice will depend upon what position(s) you play—center, forward or guard. It will do very little good for a guard to spend a lot of time practicing shots close to the basket or for a center to spend most of his time shooting 20 foot perimeter shots. Practice what you will need in game situations. First, I will explain various shooting drills you can practice. Second, I will describe four specific schedules of drills you can choose from, drills for the all-around player; for centers, for forwards, and for guards.

SHOOTING DRILLS

You should always begin your daily practice by taking a few minutes to "warm-up." By doing this, you allow your body and arms to loosen up so you don't strain them or push your shot because your muscles are still "tight." To warm-up properly, start in close to the basket and take 20 to 50 shots of different kinds. The first three shooting drills I introduce are excellent for this.

As you look over these shooting drills to pick a personal schedule for yourself, commit to *make* a set number of shots every day from each shooting drill you choose. *Make* 10 or 15 shots from each spot when you first begin. (*Remember *each drill has 2 spots,* so that will be 20-30 shots for each drill.) *Make* 10, 15, 20 or 25 from each spot. Do not exceed 25! If you practice every day, making more than 25 will not be necessary. Making 15 shots is adequate. I have emphasized *make* a specific number of shots. It will do little good if you go out and take some quick shots and do not improve. Do not get discouraged when you first begin. Something new and unfamiliar is never easy to learn. Commit to practice these drills every day for five to six days a week for a three to four-week period. I guarantee in that short time you will see a great improvement in your shooting accuracy. In one month you will be able to do them in half the time that it took you the first day.

For an extra challenge, after making your 10-15 shots from each spot, also commit to make three shots in a row and later four or five in a row before moving on to practice your next shooting drill. In quick review while you practice shooting:

(1) Warm up properly.
(2) *Make* a specific number of shots from each spot you practice every day (10, 15, 20 or 25). Each drill has two spots, one on each side of the court.
(3) For an extra challenge, commit to make three shots in a row from each spot. This will help your concentration and build your determination. Once you improve make four or five in a row.

Drill #1—Warming Up Shots

(A) Stand 3 to 5 feet away from the backboard. Shoot and make 10 shots using the backboard. (When on the right side, shoot with your right hand. On the left side of the backboard, shoot with your left hand for this drill.)
(B) Shoot and make 10 shots on the opposite side and shoot with the opposite hand. [Figure 1-1]

[1-1]

Drill #2—Lehman Drill

George Lehman, a former professional player and an "artist" at shooting the basketball, developed this drill to help players improve their shooting form. This drill takes concentration and work to develop. It is necessary in warming up properly, to practice shooting each day.

(A) Take the ball in your shooting hand holding it over

[1-2]

[1-3]

your head [Figure 1-2]. (Your non-shooting hand should be by your side.)

(B) Make sure your arm is straight as you hold the ball up [Figure 1-2]. (Do *not* allow your arm to tilt to the left or right or this will cause you to shoot the ball to the side of the rim [Figure 1-3]). Do *not* hold the ball out in front of you. This will cause you to push the ball at the rim. It will take away your ability to "arch" the ball correctly

9

[Figure 1-4]. The correct form is to hold the ball straight up and to the side of your head [Figure 1-2 and 1-5].

[1-4]   [1-5]

(C) *Concentrate* on the middle of the rim and shoot the ball. Extend your arm fully and use a good "follow-through" motion with your wrist [Figure 1-6]. Do *not* follow the flight of the ball with your eyes. Keep concentrating on the rim until your shot has gone through the basket.

[1-6]

(D) Repeat the shot. Make this shot 5 to 10 times from each of the 3 spots marked in Figure [1-7]. (This is also an excellent drill to do from the free-throw line for practice.)

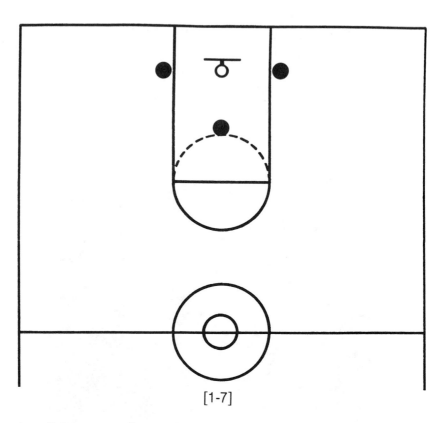

[1-7]

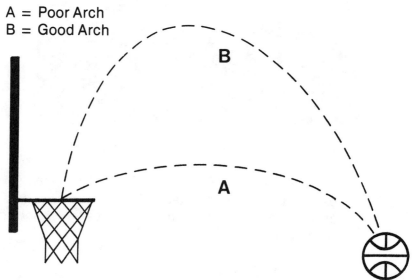

A = Poor Arch
B = Good Arch

12

[1-8]

Drill #3—Mikan Drill

George Mikan, an all-star player in the NBA and a member of the Basketball Hall of Fame, made this drill popular. It is a simple hookshot drill in close to the basket.

(A)   Stand about 3 to 5 feet to the side of the rim on the right side. Hook the ball with your right hand to make it hit inside the top corner of the square on the backboard [Figure 1-8].

(B)   Without letting the ball touch the ground after it goes through the net, grab it and, going to the left side this time, go off the opposite leg (right), hooking the ball with the left hand [Figure 1-9].

13

[1-9]

Drill #4—Baseline Pivots

This is an excellent shot and an offensive move for all centers and postplayers. It involves shooting and choreography and will take practice to develop correctly.

(A) Stand outside the lane by the closest hash mark to the baseline. *Hold the ball above your head so it cannot be stolen* [Figure 1-10].

(B) Now, pivot with your *left* foot to the baseline side of the court so that you are now facing the basket. The ball should still be above your head [Figure 1-11].

(C) Shoot the ball.

14

[1-10]

(D) Make 10 shots, then practice pivoting to the other side
     with your *right* foot to the foul-line side of the court
     and shoot the ball [Figure 1-12].

With the baseline pivot drill, the two spots you should make
10 shots from are represented by each pivot move; 10 to the left
and 10 to the right side. You should alternate to the other side of
the lane every other day when you practice this drill. This will
enable you to be effective from both sides of the court.

In a game situation, the direction you pivot will *always* be to

[1-11]

the opposite side that your defensive man is playing you. You may want to use a chair to represent a defensive player. Put it on the opposite side of your body, then the one you will be pivoting to [Figures 1-10, 1-11, 1-12].

[1-12]

Drill #5—Hook Shots

The "Hook Shot" is a great shot for any center or low post player to learn. It is extremely difficult to defend. It is shot basically the same way as the hook shot in the Mikan Drill but farther away and therefore it requires more practice. To practice hook shots:

(A) Begin in the same position with the ball as the baseline pivot drill [Figure 1-10]. Pretend you just received the ball from a team-mate.

(B) Using your left foot as a pivot foot, turn to the baseline side while taking a right handed hook shot, *without*

[1-13]

using the backboard [Figure 1-13]. In the *same motion* your left arm should be extended out toward the lane area (defensive player) to help protect your shot [Figure 1-13]. This must be done in *one motion* as one complete move, and it takes practice, otherwise you will pick up needless fouls.

(C)   Make 10 shots, then practice pivoting to the foul-line side, stepping off of your right foot and taking a lefthanded hookshot [Figure 1-14].

Each day alter which side of the court you shoot from just as in the baseline pivot drills. Remember, this is not simply a shot, it also involves choreographic movement (pivot) just like a

18

[1-14]

dancer. Unless you are willing to practice this shot hundreds of times, you will not perform it effectively. It can be learned, and it is an excellent shot. If you practice it a little each day, it will become "second nature" to you and easy to perform. But you have to work at it.

Drill #6—Free Throws

After doing primary warm-up drills (shooting drills 1-3), free throws are an excellent *secondary* warm-up drill to do before you begin taking shots which require more exertion and are more difficult [1-15].

(A) Make 10, 20 or 25 free throws after you have completed your primary warm-up drills.

(B) Make 10 free throws in-between each shooting drill you practice.

19

[1-15]

At the end of your practice each day you should shoot about 50 free throws. More than this is not necessary. You're trying to build confidence and good habits, and 50 free throws will do this. You should be able to convert over 70 percent of your free throws in games. If you are not able to do this, practice!

Drill #7—Perimeter Shots

Perimeter shots are those shots whose range extends anywhere past the foul line perimeter. The perimeter is an

20

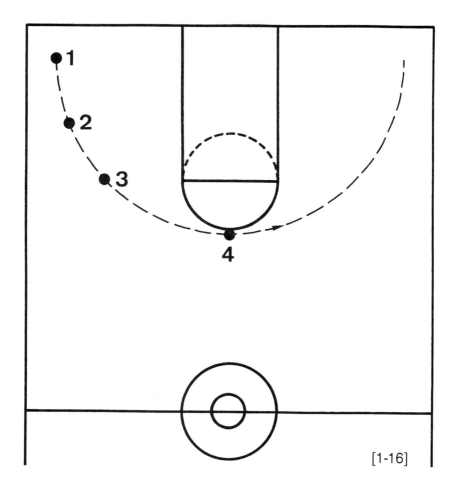

[1-16]

imaginary half circle in the offensive end of the court [Figure 1-16]. A player's perimeter area is the area farthest away from the basket that he can effectively and consistently (50 percent or more) make his shots. Perimeter shots can be taken as a jump shot or set shot depending on the preference and abilities of the individual player.

There are four basic perimeter shots:
(1)   Baseline shots [Figure 1-16, #1].
(2)   Bank shots [Figure 1-16, #2] from this angle use the backboard to "bank" the shot in.

[1-17]

(3) Wing shots [Figure 1-16, #3].

(4) Straight-away shots [Figure 1-16, #4]. In taking this shot you only need to shoot from *1 spot* or make 10 shots. (All other perimeter shots have 2 spots—one on each side of the court.)

(A) Begin with the ball in your baseline perimeter. You should be facing the basketball with the ball in your hands.

(B) Take your shot, follow and retrieve the rebound. Then dribble with the hand closest to the baseline side of the court over to your perimeter area on the opposite side of the court.

(C) Again face the basket with the ball in your hands as if you just received a pass from a teammate.

(D) Take your shot [Figure 1-17]. Follow and retrieve your rebound and dribble with the hand closest to the baseline side of the court. Take all your shots in this manner until you have made 20 total or 10 from each side.

(E)   Repeat the process for bank shots, wing shots, etc.

Being able to shoot effectively from any of these perimeter areas will give you the ability to score from any position on the court.

[1-18]

Drill #8—Jump Shots off the Dribble

(A)   Begin with the ball in your hands facing the basket.
(B)   Holding the ball in front of you, fake with the ball to the left [Figure 1-18].

[1-19]

(C) Then in the same motion go to the right with the ball, taking 1 to 2 dribbles as you step to the right away from the defensive player (use a chair) [Figure 1-19].

[D] Stop quickly with your body "squared away" (facing the basket) and in the same motion go up on balance for your shot [Figure 1-20]. Do not jump too far forward, to the side or fade away.

[E] Make 10 shots faking left, then going to your right. Then make 10 shots faking right, then going to your

24

[1-20]

left for a jumpshot.

[F] Each day change the spot you practice your 20 shots from so that you are comfortable in all three areas of the court [Figure 1-21].

If you have practiced your other perimeter shots, you already have the ability to shoot well from this range. You only need to develop the choreography to take jump shots off the drible. The important thing is to be able to go both to your left and right side equally well.

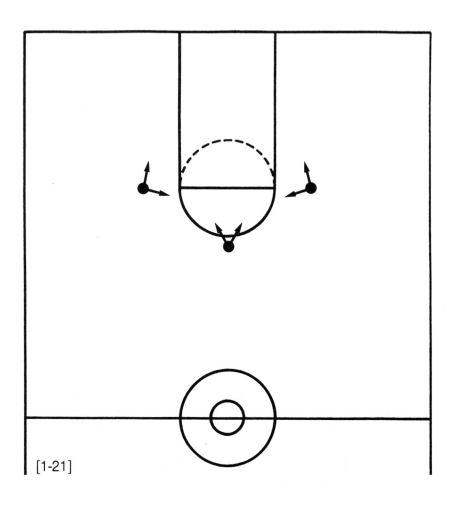

[1-21]

Drill #9—The "Tap" Drill

The "Tap" Drill is excellent for centers and forwards. It can also be beneficial to guards. It is designed to help you be a better offensive rebounder and develop control of the ball with one hand when rebounding. Many times there will be rebounds you cannot reach with both hands. This drill will help you to develop the ability to 'tap' the ball to a place where you can get better control of it or enable you to tap it into the basket. How to practice the tap drill:

(A) Take the ball in your right hand holding it over your

26

[1-22]   [1-23]

head. (You should be facing the backboard and be 2 to 3 feet away.)

(B) Using your right hand toss the ball high against the backboard. As you *jump up* fully extending your arm and body, tap it against the backboard again for 5 or 10 repetitions [Figure 1-22].

(C) After every 5 or 10 repetitions, tap the ball into the basket [Figure 1-23].

(D) After doing 2 to 3 sets of 10, or 5 to 6 sets of 5, switch to the other side of the backboard and use the left

hand to repeat the process.
(*You should be using your fingertips to control the ball. Do not let the ball touch the palms of your hand.)

Workout Schedules for Drills

Drills for the All Around Player

Drill #1   Warm-up shots
Drill #2   Lehmann Drill
Drill #3   Mikan Drill
—25 free throws
Drill #9   "Tap" Drill
—10 free throws
Drill #7   Perimeter shots Drill
—10 free throws
Drill #8   Jump shots off the dribble
—10 free throws

Drills for Centers

Since centers spend most of their time close to the basket, they should spend most of their time in shooting practice close to the basket. A good ratio consists of 80 percent of your shots being taken close around the basket and 20 percent of your shots out away from the basket for when you need to play a high post position. These percentages are found in game situations. (These do *not* include free throws. Everybody should practice free throws.)

Drill #1   Warm-up shots
Drill #2   Lehmann Drill
Drill #3   Mikan Drill
—25 free throws
Drill #4   Baseline Pivots Drill
—10 free throws
Drill #5   Hook shots Drill
—10 free throws
Drill #7   (*Note—straight-away shots *only*. Make 25 jump or set shots from the high post perimeter at the foul line or above.)

—10 free throws
Drill #9   Tap Drill

Drills for Forwards

Forwards are required to perform well both inside and outside. I suggest you follow the workout schedule for the "All around player" (page 20) if you are a small forward. If you are a strong-power forward, follow the same workout except switch Drill #8 and replace it with Drill #4 or Drill #5, *with whichever you feel most comfortable. As a strong forward you will need to be very good with the ball around the basket. Either of these drills will give you this ability.*

Drills for Guards

Drill #1   Warm-up shots
Drill #2   Lehmann Drill
Drill #3   Mikan Drill
—25 free throws
Drill #7   Perimeter shots Drill
—10 free throws
Drill #8   Jump shots off the dribble
—10 free throws

The drills you use as a player or coach to fulfill your needs are up to you. Whatever you do, keep this thought in mind: "Quality time is more valuable than Quantity time."

This means you are better practicing and becoming excellent in a few areas, rather than average at many. One or two hours practicing specific drills is more valuable than spending four hours "just shooting" or playing in uncompetitive scrimmages. I have seen many players go to gym to "shoot" and spend three or four hours taking trick shots or playing in "pick-up" games. You will gain more and go farther if you spend one or two hours a day practicing specific drills.

When I served as a missionary for The Church of Jesus Christ of Latter-day Saints, Hyrum Smith, my mission president, had a saying:

Success—When the successful person is willing to do that which the unsuccessful person is *not* willing to do.

If you want to develop the "art" of shooting or of any other skills in basketball, spend *quality* time. Be willing to do what the unsuccessful basketball player is not willing to do—practice for a specific purpose.

COACHES CHALK TALK

At the end of each chapter I will dedicate a small section entitled "Coaches Chalk Talk." My purpose is to suggest ways to implement the skills and ideas discussed into a team-oriented practice. As a coach and player myself, I know there are hundreds of ways to teach demonstrate every phase and skill of the game. All coaches have learned how to teach different skills for other coaches, from what they read, and from what they did as players.

I am not suggesting that the drills I introduce are better than those you now know and use. They are extremely effective and efficient. I have seen them produce superb results, improving players and team skills, building confidence and consistency. The fact that you are reading this book suggests you are open to new ideas and willing to learn and improve.

In talking about shooting, let me first ask a question. Does your team consistently shoot below 50 percent from the floor and 70 percent from the free throw line? Three things are absolutely critical for a player to have his full "potential" of skills and confidence in shooting during a basketball season. First, shooting must be practiced each and *every day* of team practice. Second, players should practice the same shots the same way *every day.* Third, the shots they practice should be directly applicable to where you have them in game situations. (Suggestions on what shots players of each position should practice are found on pages 20-21.)

These three things are critical because of the "Law of Familiarity." This states: "The more often we do a specific action the more comfortable, confident and proficient we will be when doing it." That is why it is better to practice the same shooting drills 5 to 6 days a week than to practice 2 or 3 different types of drills two days of the week or to only practice shooting drills 2 or 3 days of the week. This is especially true during the basketball season.

Depending on your facilities and the size of your team, shooting drills can best be practiced in two ways:

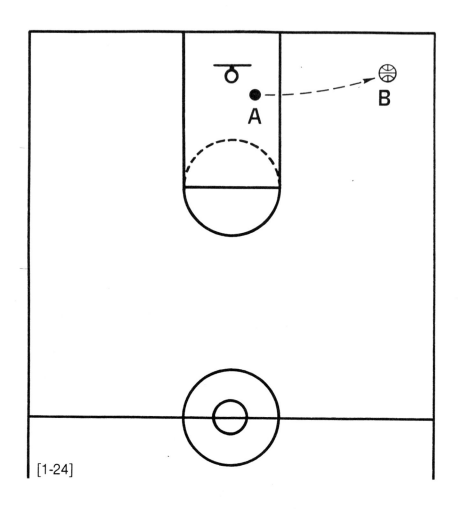

[1-24]

(1) *Two players using one ball* [Figure 1-24]. Player "A"
rebounds and player "B" shoots. Do not switch until
after player "B" *makes* his shots; otherwise, it is
difficult to develop a "shooting rhythm" or "feel"
from the spot he is practicing. After player "B" makes
his 10 or 15 shots, he rebounds, and player "A"
shoots. Then move to the next practice spot.

(2) *Three players using two balls* [Figure 1-25]. Player
"A" shoots ball 1, player "B" rebounds and passes to
player "C." Player "C" passes ball 2 to player "A,"

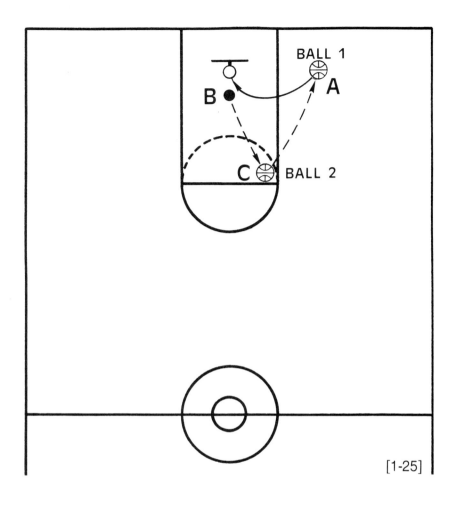

BALL 1

B

A

C — BALL 2

[1-25]

then receives ball 1 from player "B." This motion keeps going until player "A" makes his 10 to 15 shots, then all players rotate 1 position. This is the fastest way to do shooting drills in a team practice.

It is better to have a player make a specific number of shots. It makes him concentrate more and puts a little pressure on him not to slow down the other players. If he is just allowed "to shoot" for 3-5 minutes, often he will not work hard.

Players of these positions—center, forward, guard—should have three to four basic shots they practice *each* day with two spots for each shooting drill. This should take 20 to 30 minutes of your practice time each day. If you need to extend your daily practice 15 minutes a day, then do it. The few extra minutes you invest will bring you great dividends. All players like to shoot, and they will enjoy and appreciate the practice.

A thought which I will reiterate throughout this book is this: To effectively implement and teach correct basketball skills, first realize that for many of your players, what you will have them practice may be totally new and unfamiliar to them. Even the players you have returning at the beginning of the season may not have practiced these skills since last year. Understand this and allow for an hour of extra practice time in the first two weeks of the new season. Use the two weeks as your "pre-season preparation period."

Once the players have practiced these things *every day* for two weeks, they will perform more effectively, efficiently and in a lot less time. Then as the season develops, you can cut your practices back to 1½ or 2½ hours, depending on your objectives. Remember, if you are not willing to take the extra time to teach them correctly, do *not* expect them to perform effectively and efficiently. I close with this thought:

You *enjoy* the price of success, you *pay* the price of failure.

Spend an extra 30 minutes a day to enjoy the price of success!

THE "ART" OF BALLHANDLING

You have to know the things fundamentally . . . like a dancer, you've rehearsed so many times you don't go out and worry about making mistakes. . .

Oscar Robertson

—N.B.A. Rookie of the Year 1960-61
—N.B.A. All-Star Team
—N.B.A. M.V.P. 1963-64
*—Milwaukee Bucks World Champions
  1970-71*
—Most career assists in N.B.A. (9,887)
—Member of Basketball Hall of Fame

2

THE "ART" OF BALL-HANDLING

In this chapter you can learn:

> Good ball-handling is an essential skill for great players. Here are some ball-handling objectives that will dramatically enhance your skill:
> - 20 drills to develop exceptional dribbling and quickness
> - 15 advanced drills for greater dexterity and coordination.
> - Ball-handling you can practice as you watch T.V.
> - Extra effective team drills

The most neglected skill in the game of basketball is ball-handling. Think about it! Most turnovers and mistakes happen as a result of poor ball-handling, such as double dribble, traveling, "palming" or carrying the ball over. A player who dribbles with his eyes down or having to glance down at the ball often commits a charging foul or misses the easy pass he could have thrown. Passes that go astray because of "bad hands" or a poor choice of a pass are a result of poor ball-handling skills.

In basketball, while shooting is first, the second skill of the game that is really an art is ball-handling. A player who knows how to handle a basketball properly can be very graceful and artistic. A great example of the art of ball-handling are the

Harlem Globetrotters. They are world renowned for their abilities of ball-handling, not of shooting. Before crowds all over the world they perform feats that amaze and captivate their audiences. They have rehearsed thousands of times. They practice these skills over and over using the same choreography every day.

If you do not believe ball-handling is an art, ask yourself these questions:

—How many players can dribble a ball with their left and right hand equally well?

—How many players can dribble full-speed without having to look down at the ball?

—How many can use a "jab step" dribble to drive through an opening?

—How many players going full-speed can, without losing pace or looking down, change direction with a reverse pivot, between the legs or behind the back dribble while protecting the ball?

—How many players have a left side or weak dribbling hand which makes them ineffective and uncomfortable?

These are all basic ball-handling and dribbling skills. I coached in high school and worked many basketball camps from California with John Wooden to Massachusetts with "Red" Auerbach. Seldom have I seen ball-handling and dribbling fundamentals taught properly. I remember one basketball camp where there was a ball-handling lecture for thirty minutes in the morning. The counselors (all were college and "pro" players) literally had to "cast lots" to see who would give the demonstration. None of them had enough knowledge and confidence to teach fundamental skills of ball-handling for thirty minutes.

Some coaches act as if ball-handling is not so important. Perhaps they were never taught these skills properly, so it is something they do not know how to teach. They lack the knowledge and skills to teach this phase of the gameproperly and with confidence. A coach may be embarrassed or scared to show that he does not know.

But every coach loves a player who can break a full court press on his own or control a fast break quickly and effectively. All coaches love a player who can see the whole court and give soft, accurate passes. When a player makes a ball-handling error, however, the player gets the blame for something he was never taught to do.

Ball-handling gives an added dimension to any team. It adds another problem for the opposing team. How many fast breaks do you see run only by passes? How many teams do you see win without an effective fast break? The game is changing. Players today are bigger, stronger, and faster. Shot clocks are being used by everyone—professional, international, college and some high schools. It makes basketball a faster, more exciting paced game.

Whatever drills you choose should relate to what you use or need on the basketball court. How many ball-handling "tricks" can you use in a real game? Hardly any, and if you do not want to always sit on the bench, probably none. To be able to spin the ball on your fingers, or dribble in "figure eights" two inches off the ground, or any other fancy tricks or shots with the ball is okay. But it is not half as beneficial or important as to develop specific dribbling moves. Reverse pivots, jab steps, behind the back, between the legs dribbling, to change directions and more—all of these are directly applicable to game situations. They are choreographic moves which, when rehearsed over and over, become "second nature" and can be used properly, effectively and artistically in game situations. It is like practicing a dance routine over and over until you can do it naturally. It becomes a part of your repertoire, and it can be both beautiful and effective.

By becoming a good ball-handler you not only develop important skills to use in the game, you also develop confidence. The more skills you develop, the more confidence you will have and the more valuable you will be to your team. A coach loves a great shooter, but if he has a great shooter who can dribble and pass the ball well, then that player has tripled his value to the coach and to the team. He has multiplied his chances of playing, especially if there are other great shooters on the team!

Dribbling and ball-handling are the most difficult skills to master. They take the most exertion to practice. That is why it is better to practice half an hour to an hour *every day* than to practice four hours one day and none the next. Do not burn yourself out. Be consistent. By doing a little *each day* you will develop great ball-handling skills, confidence and determination. Decide on what you want to practice. Be consistent in striving for it every day.

"It's the little drops of rain that fill the water barrel, one drop at a time."

By doing a little each day, your talent will gradually and consistently grow, and you will find confidence and success.

DRIBBLING AND BALL-HANDLING DRILLS

Three objectives for ball-handling and dribbling drills:

(1) *Dribble with your head and eyes up.* This will enable you to see the whole court and keep you from committing needless fouls and turnovers.

(2) *Develop a "feel" for the ball.* Work and work at these drills until the ball "feels" like part of your hand, until it feels as if it fits your hand like a glove. Once you develop a feel for the basketball, you will never need to look down while dribbling. The ball will be like a magnet always being drawn to its proper place—*your hand!*

(3) *Use your fingertips to control the ball.* Do not allow the ball to ever touch the palms of your hands; it will make the basketball more difficult to control.

Dribbling and ball-handling drills are divided into five sections.

1. Full court dribbling drills
2. "Closet drills" for dribbling
3. Maravich ball-handling drills
4. "T.V." drills
5. Tips to help improve your ball-handling skills

1. Full-Court Dribbling Drills

Although the best place to practice basketball is in a gym and the best place to practice "full court dribbling drills" is on a full-length court, it isn't the only way. I have practiced these drills in school hallways after school or in the street, pretending the distance between two telephone poles was my court. I have even practiced using tennis and racquetball courts, pretending I dribbled to half court and then back to the baseline. All you need is some room, a basketball and imagination. If you do not have access to an indoor or outdoor basketball court, use a hallway, sidewalk or street, but whatever you do, *do not* use an excuse.

Rules for full-court dribbling drills

(1) *Pick a spot.* Pick a spot on the wall at the opposite end of the court [Figure 2-1]. Keep your eyes on this spot as you dribble. This will train you to keep your eyes up as you dribble and to see the whole court.

[2-1]

[2-2]

(2) *Full-speed.* Do all drills at full-speed. *Do it as fast as you can while dribbling with good control.* Dribbling the ball, you may be slow at first, but you will improve as you practice. To begin, get your footwork (choreography) down. Speed will come as you work hard.

(3) *Hip height.* Never dribble the ball higher than your hips. (Your hips are *not* your waist; your waist is higher.) This will give much better control of the ball.

(4) *Stay low.* When you are dribbling (reverse pivot, between legs, jab step), bend your knees and get lower. This will give you more balance, better control and more quickness in these moves.

(5) *One set.* As you do these drills, one time means to go to the opposite endline and return. Do each drill a minimum of 3 times and a maximum of 5 times.

RIGHT HAND

(A) Begin on the end line of the court [Figure 2-5, spot "A"].

(B) Dribble the ball to the opposite end line and back 3 times.

(C) As you dribble the ball fullspeed, keep it ahead of you to the right side of your body [Figure 2-3].

(*Note: If you are right-handed, work hard to develop your left hand and vice-versa. Do the left hand drill *twice*, before and after you do the right hand drill.)

LEFT HAND

(A) Same way as the right hand but on the opposite side.

JAB STEP

A "jab" step is a move that allows you to fake out a defender without having to change hands or direction.

(A) Begin dribbling with your right hand, go rapidly to the extended foul line [Figure 2-5, line I].

(B) When you get to this line, with your left foot, "jab" or step quickly to your left side [Figure 2-3]. After you jab with your left foot, use it to "push off," making your body go back to the right [Figure 2-4].

(C) Continue dribbling fullspeed and repeat the move at lines II, III, and IV [Figure 2-5], going both directions of the court.

[2-3]

[2-4]

(D) Do 2 times with right and 2 times with left hand.

(E) Your steps should be similar to those in [Figure 2-6].

(*Note: Do not overextend by jabbing too far and losing balance. You only need to jab about 12 inches to the side to fake out the defender.)

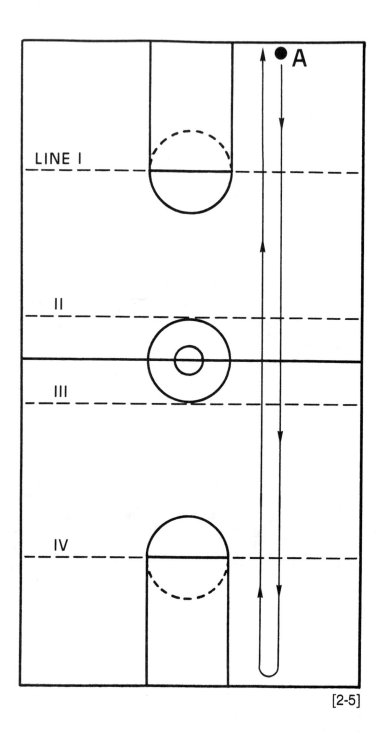

LINE I

II

III

IV

A

[2-5]

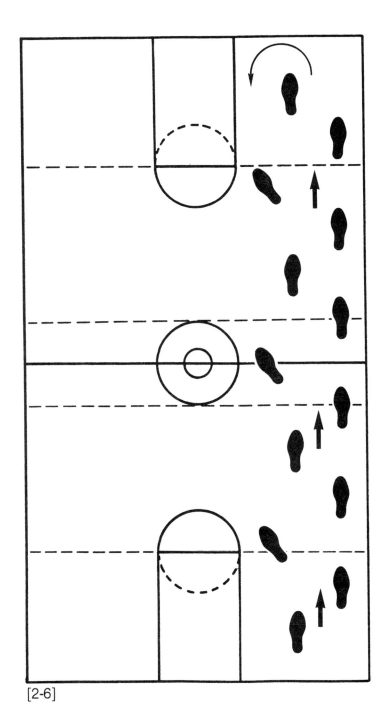

[2-6]

BETWEEN-THE-LEGS DRIBBLE

The between-the-legs dribble enables a player to change his direction without having to dribble the ball in front of him or turn his back to the basket. It is effective and quick and allows the dribbler to protect the ball.

(A) Begin at the end-line dribbling full speed with your right hand to line I [Figure 2-5].

(B) When you get to line I, dribble through your legs. (The ball should always go from front to back [Figure 2-7].)

(C) As the hand receiving the ball touches, immediately push the ball forward and head in a forward direction [Figure 2-8]. Now repeat with your left hand.

(D) Go full speed to lines II, III, and IV [Figure 2-5], repeating the move at each line as you change directions each time [Figures 2-9, 2-10].

(E) Do the drill 2 to 3 times.

[2-7]

[2-8]

47

[2-9]

[2-10]

48

"REVERSE PIVOT" DRIBBLE

This is a dribbling move used to change direction, especially effective when a defensive player is overplaying you to one side of the court, or you are heading toward a sideline or baseline while being defended. This move is exactly what the name says, a "pivot" to the reverse or opposite side.

(A) Begin at the end line, with your right hand dribble full-speed to line 1 [Figure 2-3].

(B) Then plant your *left* foot and privot your body ¾ of the way around toward the left, while keeping the ball at your right hand and *no higher than your knees* [Figure 2-11]. Your last dribble before pivoting should be low with your right hand meeting the ball at knee level and keeping contact with it until you complete the pivot.

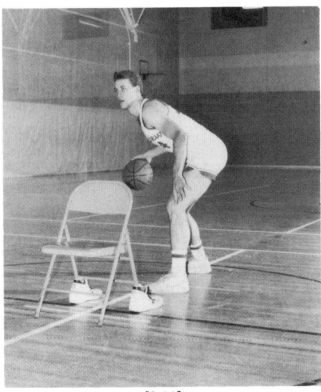

[2-11]

(C) As you complete the pivot, allow the ball to "drop" from your hand [Figure 2-12]. Your left hand should then dribble the ball as you go in the other direction [Figure 2-13].

(D) Advance to lines II, III, and IV [Figure 2-5], changing direction at each line, as you use both hands to pivot both ways.

(E) Do the drill 2 to 3 times.

[2-12]

50

[2-13]

BEHIND THE BACK DRIBBLE

This allows you to change directions while avoiding a defensive player in the open court and without losing your momentum and speed. It can be very useful in fast break situations.

(A) As you dribble, "swing" the ball around your waist, pushing it ahead of your body as you move forward [Figure 2-14].

(B) Do the drill 2 to 3 times.

[2-14]

BETWEEN-THE-LEGS WALK
("2 bounce" and "1 bounce")

Although these two drills are not directly applicable to game situations, the benefits from practicing them are. These are *walking* drills and will help in three ways:

(1) Help you to concentrate on keeping your head and eyes up (pick a spot on the wall).

(2) Help you develop a better "feel" in handling the ball.

(3) Help you practice your choreography for the Between-the-Legs speed dribble more rapidly.

"2" Bounce Walk

(A) Take 1 dribble ("1 bounce") with the left hand, then with the next dribble ("2 bounce"), dribble the ball through your legs going from front to back [Figure 2-15]. Without stopping take your next dribble with your right hand ("1 bounce") [Figure 2-16], the the next dribble through your legs ("2 bounce"), again going from front to back [Figure 2-17].

(B) Continue this move as you walk up the court and back.

(C) Do drill 2 to 3 times.

[215]

[2-16]

53

[2-17]

"1" Bounce Walk

This drill is done with your legs moving in a scissor motion as you walk forward. It is done the same as the "2 bounce" drill except you use "1 bounce."

(A) Dribble alternating each hand with every new bounce. Each dribble goes in a front to back scissor motion between your legs [Figures 2-14, 2-15].

(B) Repeat without stopping. Do the drill 2 to 3 times.

54

2. Closet Drills

You may not have access to a gym but want to improve your dribbling skills. You need very little room to do them, that is why I call them "closet drills." They are perfect for the player who does not have good facilities, but does have the will to work. These drills can be done in basements, driveways, garages, sidewalks, patios, roof terraces, closets and even in gyms! They can be done in any weather, sun, rain, wind or snow. You only need desire and a basketball. Closet drills are excellent practice for dribbling and half court situations in a game, running down the clock, directing control offenses, and delay games. I did not create all of these drills, but I use them all and this enabled me to play and not sit on the bench. If you do not want to sit on the bench when the basketball season begins, do not sit down in the off-season. Work, it's that simple.

Rules for "Closet Drills"

(1) *Knee height.* Never dribble any higher than your knees. This will give you quicker reactions and better ball control. Bend your knees, *not* your back so you can keep your head up.

(2) *Pick a spot.* Pick a spot to look at on the wall, a tree, pole or house. Keep your eyes on it as you practice. Do *not* watch the ball.

(3) *Work hard.* Concentrate and develop speed at doing these drills. If you are lazy in practice, you will not have quick reactions in game situations.

LEFT HAND

(A) Stand in a *low* position, knees bent and left hand extended to the side as you dribble [Figure 2-18].

(B) Dribble the ball in a "4 spot" half circle motion [Figure 2-19].

(C) Each time you complete half circle equals "one time." Do 25 times.

(D) If the left hand is your weak hand, do the drill twice.

RIGHT HAND

(A) Do as the left hand drill.

[2-18]

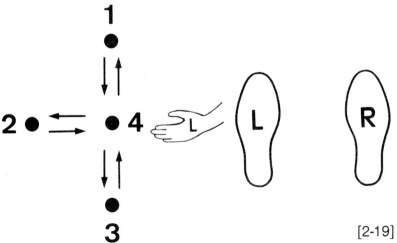

[2-19]

JAB STEP

(A) Do this drill the same way as the full court drill but stay in one area [Figures 2-5, 2-6]. Jab then stay low and take a couple of dribbles and jab again. One jab equals 1 time.

(B) Do 25 times for both the left and right hand.

BETWEEN LEGS "2 BOUNCE" SPEED DRILL

(A) Stay low with your head up. Dribble no higher than your knees. Dribble once with your left hand ("1 bounce"); then dribble through your legs [Figure 2-20] ("2 bounce"), then dribble once with your right hand [Figure 2-21] ("1 bounce") and then dribble through your legs ("2 bounce") [Figure 2-22], etc.

(B) Repeat the drill without stopping as fast as you can.

(C) Do the drill 25 times.

[2-20] [2-21]

BETWEEN LEGS "1 BOUNCE" SPEED DRILL

(A) Do the same way as 2-bounce drill but use only "1" bounce for each dribble between the legs as you move your legs in a scissor motion [Figures 2-20, 2-22].

(B) Do the drill 25 times.

[2-22]

SHUFFLE DRIBBLE

This is an excellent drill to develop coordination, quickness and lateral movement. Do it the same as the "2 bounce" drill except instead of moving your legs in a front-to-back scissor motion, move them left to right and right to left in a lateral motion.

(A) Dribble through your legs as you move laterally (sideways) left to right 1 step [Figure 2-23]. Dribble once with your right hand [Figure 2-24]. Dribble through your legs as you move laterally right to left 1 step in the opposite direction [Figure 2-25]. Dribble once with your left hand; repeat drill without stopping.

(B) Do 25 times as fast as you can.

[2-23]

[2-24]

"2 BOUNCE" WALK

(A) Do the same as between legs "2 bounce" speed drill except walk in place as you stand straight up. Move legs in a front to back scissor motion.

(B) Do it 25 times.

"1 BOUNCE" WALK

(A) Same as "2 bounce" walk except with the bounce going through your legs each time.

60

[2-25]

3. Maravich Ball-Handling Drills

"Pistol" Pete Maravich, the all-time scoring leader in NCAA basketball history and All-Star NBA player, developed and made popular most of these drills. They are designed to help improve your ball-handling skills, coordination, quickness, and strength and endurance in your arms and hands, excellent drills to learn if you want extra practice or have a lot of extra time. You can do these *anywhere*. (*Note: Do not do these drills until *after* you practice your dribbling and shooting drills each day. Those drills are directly applicable to game situations. Maravich drills are helpful and great to learn but as a secondary workout, not your primary workout.)

Do the drills rapidly. Do all drills a minimum of 10 times.

(A) *Slaps.* Holding the ball in front of your chest "slap" the ball hard as you move the ball back and forth between your left and right hand.

(B) *Pinch.* Holding the ball in your right hand "pinch" it toward your left hand using all 5 fingers. Then with the left hand pinch toward your right hand; go back and forth.

(C) *Taps.* Hold ball over your head with your arms fully extended. Tap the ball back and forth between your fingertips.

(D) *Circles.* [Figures 2-26, 2-27, 2-28] After tap drill, bring the ball down and going in a clockwise direction move it in a circle motion around your:

  1. Head
  2. Waist
  3. Both ankles (stand with ankles together)
  4. Right ankle (stand with ankles apart)
  5. Left ankle

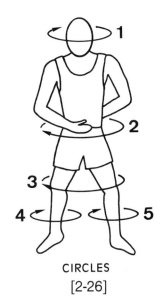

CIRCLES
[2-26]

[2-27]   [2-28]

Then reverse your direction going in a counter-clockwise circle motion as you move the ball back up from your ankles to your head.

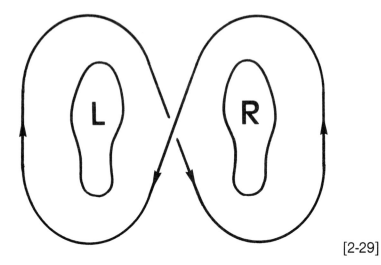

[2-29]

(E) *Figure 8's* [Figure 2-29]. Hold the ball at knee level. Keep your feet stationary and apart. Pass the ball in and out of your legs in a "figure 8" motion. Do it passing in a front-to-back motion, then change and go back-to-front.

[2-30]

(F) *Scissors* [Figures 2-30, 2-31]. Hold the ball at knee level. Pass the ball in between your legs as you move your legs in a scissor motion. Do it in both directions.

[2-31]

(G) *Rhythm Drill.* Hold the ball in front of you below your knees, with your feet apart. Swing ball around behind right ankle catching it in between your legs with your left hand in front, and your right hand in back [Figure 2-32]. Let ball bounce *only* once as your hands switch positions (right hand in front, left in back) [Figure 2-33]. Swing ball all the way around your body to the back again and repeat the move. Do the drill in both directions.

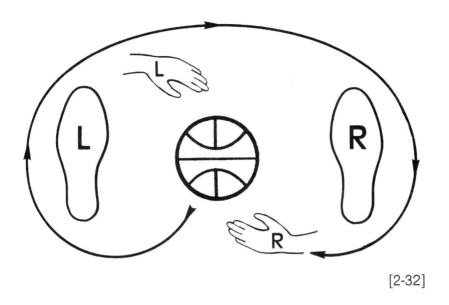

[2-32]

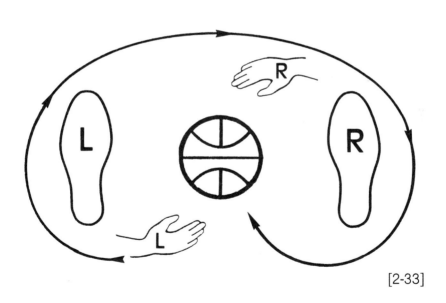

[2-33]

(H) *Flop* [Figures 2-34, 2-35]. Hold the ball in front of your legs with the left hand in front, right hand in back. Keep your feet stationary. Without letting the ball hit the floor, quickly switch position of your hands. Repeat switching position of hands again quickly.

Flop

[2-34]

[2-35]

Flip

[2-36]

(l) *Flip* [Figures 2-36, 2-37]. Hold the ball in front of legs with both hands. Keep your feet stationary. "Flip" it through your legs to the back and catch it with both hands. Flip to the front again. Repeat.

[2-37]

Ball-handling Drills with a Dribble

(A) Low figure 8's dribble [Figure 2-38].

Do the same motion as figure 8's passing drill [Figure 2-27] except keep the ball as *low* to the ground as possible while dribbling many times quickly. Keep feet stationary. Do drill in *both* directions.

71

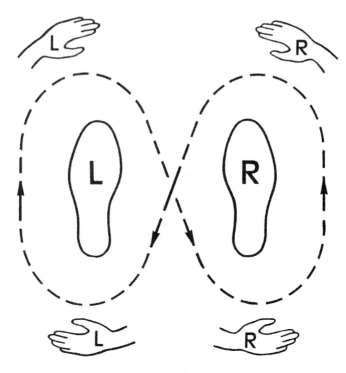

Low figure 8's dribble

[2-38]

(B) Stationary "2 bounce" drill [Figure 2-39].
   Do same as "2 bounce" closet drill (page 57) except keep the feet *stationary*. Take one bounce of the ball with left hand, one bounce through *front of legs*, one bounce with the right hand, one bounce through front of legs. Repeat quickly. Do drill in both directions also dribbling through back of legs.

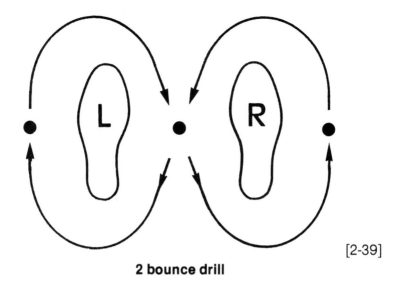

2 bounce drill

[2-39]

(C) Stationary ''1 bounce'' drill [Figure 2-40].
   Do as stationary 2 bounce drill except use only *1 bounce* to
   dribble through your legs. Do *not* dribble the ball any other
   times. Do drill in both directions.

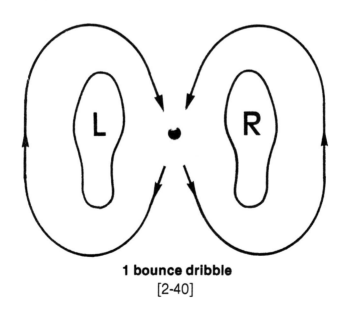

1 bounce dribble
[2-40]

(D) One-hand Circles [Figure 2-41].
Put your feet apart and keep stationary. Dribble ball around right ankle using right hand *only*. Switch to left side and left ankle. Do drill clockwise, then counter clockwise.

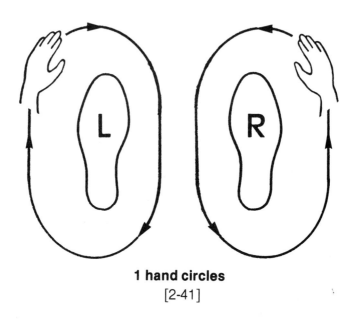

1 hand circles
[2-41]

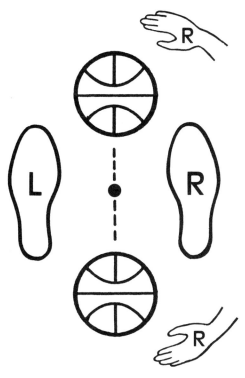

Reaction dribble

[2-42]

(E) Reaction Dribble [Figure 2-42].
Keep feet stationary and shoulder width apart. Bounce ball back and forth in between your legs using your right hand. Let ball bounce only one time. Switch hands and practice drill with left.

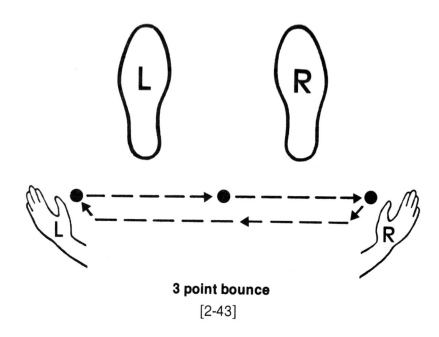

3 point bounce

[2-43]

(F) 3-Point Bounce [Figure 2-43].
Stand stationary with feet apart. Dribbling *behind* your back, bounce ball once on your right side, once behind your back, once on left side, once behind your back; repeat quickly.

(G) 4-Point Bounce [Figure 2-44].

Stand stationary with feet apart. Tap the ball once in front of your legs with right hand, once with left hand, once in back with right hand, once with left hand. Repeat quickly. Keep the ball low and in the middle of your legs.

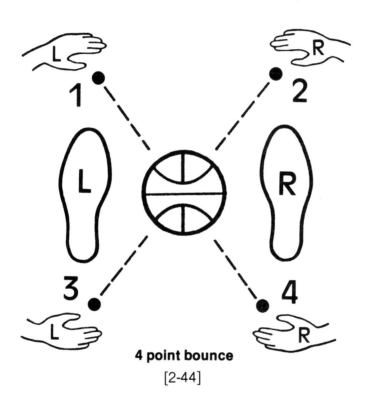

4 point bounce

[2-44]

4. TV Drills

These drills allow you to watch TV while keeping your mind on your goal—becoming a better basketball player. Keep a ball in your hands all the time you watch TV; this will help you develop a better feel for the ball. Do the drills during commercials or breaks in the program. Practice a different drill at every break. If you watch TV for 2 hours and do nothing, you have wasted 20 minutes of time you could use during commercials!

(A) *Shoot* [Figure 2-45]. Lie back on the floor and shoot the ball into the air fully extending your arm, use a lot of "follow through." This will help improve your follow through motion and help build endurance and strength in your arms. Do 25 to 50 times.

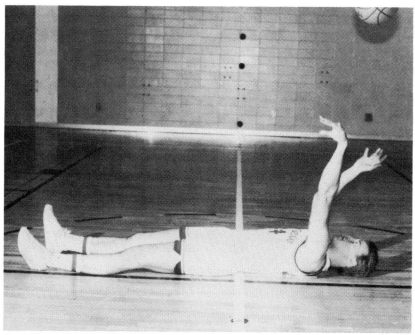

[2-45]

(B) *Chair drop* [Figures 2-46, 2-47]. Sit forward in chair. Hold ball with both hands above knees with legs apart. Drop the ball between legs, catching it with both hands behind legs. Do not let it hit the floor. Toss ball up above knees, catching it again with both hands, as rapidly as possible.

[2-46]

[2-47]

(C) *Hand Rolls* [Figure 2-48]. Hold ball in palm of your right hand. Roll your hand around the ball *without letting the ball drop or removing your fingers from the ball.* Do clockwise, then counterclockwise. Practice with both hands.

[2-48]

(D) Body Development.
1. Fingertip push-ups [Figure 2-49]. Do as many as you can. This will strengthen your fingers, wrist and arms for shooting.
2. Sit-ups. Do 50 sit-ups.

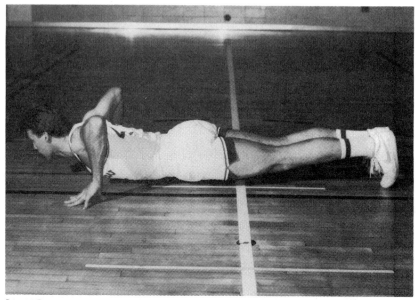

[2-49]

3. Heel lifts [Figure 2-50]. Stand arms length away from wall, facing it. Use fingertips to touch wall for balance. Extend up *all* the way on your toes, fully extending your calves, then back down. Do *not* allow heels to touch ground. Do 100 with both legs, 50 with right leg, 50 with left leg (other leg should not be touching the ground) 2-4 sets of 50 for each leg. Do 100 more for both legs (200 total). After, stretch your calves by standing flat-footed. Lean your shoulders in to touch the wall, keeping your legs straight; do *not* bend

[2-50]

knees. (*Excellent for strengthening calves and building jumping ability.)

5. Tips

(A) *Walk with head and eyes up.* Wherever you go all during the day, keep your head and eyes up as you walk. Excellent training to develop your peripheral vision and ability to see the whole court.

(B) *Use opposite hand.* Whatever you do, do it with your opposite or weak hand. (If you are right-handed, use your left hand.) Eating your meals, brushing your teeth, opening doors, flushing the toilet, even to write letters. This will build your ability and confidence to use both hands on the court and will take no extra time from your daily schedule.

(C) *Mental prep.* Write a list of things you want to do when you play. Read them through one at a time, close your eyes as you mentally picture yourself doing it correctly. Do this before you go to bed at night.

(D) *Carry a ball.* Everywhere you go (except church) carry a ball with you. To your friends', to school, to a move, everywhere!

(E) *Run and dribble.* Dribble the ball as you jog with your weak hand.

COACHES CHALK TALK

I have had more than 25 coaches in my playing career. Only one of them had me practice ball-handling regularly and taught it to me correctly. I can remember many of them putting out the balls and saying, "Okay, dribble to the other end and back two times right and left-handed." That was it, and it only happened once or twice a season! I do not ever remember seeing a whole team, except on the professional level, that could dribble the ball without a "double dribble," "traveling" or "palming the ball" being called. I do remember seeing many teams in trouble when their only ball-handling guard was hurt or fouled out. If you have been coaching for a while, you, too, have had this experience. Most players have poor ball-handling skills.

A team can cut their turnovers by 30 to 50 percent if their players develop good ball-handling skills. I am not talking about an entire team being able to dribble and pass like Bob Cousy, "Pistol" Pete Maravich, Larry Bird, "Magic" Johnson or Isaiah Thomas. All players should dribble well with both their left and right hands while having their head and eyes up to see the whole court. This is a realistic goal. It only takes practice. If you are willing to take 10 to 15 minutes of practice time a day, you can increase your players' skills, confidence, endurance, stamina and your team's overall performance.

The great thing is you can use these drills in place of some you now use, whether to warm-up your players or condition them. Full court dribbling drills are excellent for conditioning and replace a lot of sprints or running.

How to use in practice:

Full-court dribbling drills.

Depending on the number of players you have, put them in 4 lines and *no more* than 5 lines across the endline (unless you have more space to the side) [Figure 2-51]. Each line should have a minimum of 2 players and a maximum of 3 players.

Have them do all the full-court dribbling drills on pages 40-54 three to four times each to the opposite end line and back.

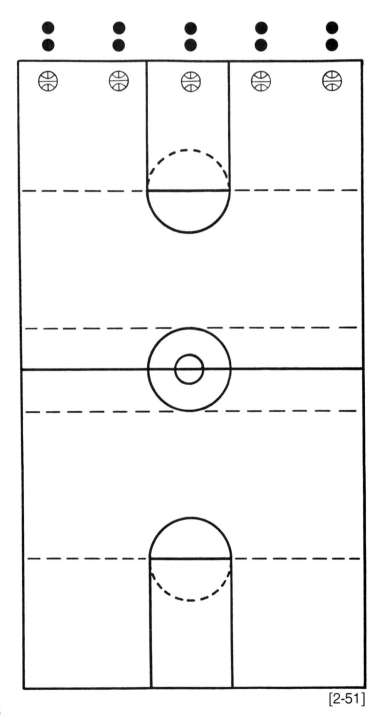

Head and eyes should be kept *up*. After all players in each line finish the drill, rotate to next drill.

Closet dribbling drills.

These are excellent to warm up players at the beginning of practice. Using the same lines, have the first man in each line step to the extended foul line. Have them do 25 repetitions with their heads up. Rotate players after each drill.

These closet drills, when done rapidly, are very good for conditioning the legs and improving players' ball-handling, quickness and coordination. (*Note: Time in team practice is valuable; it may not always be feasible to use closet drills because of time, but if you can, they will bring great benefits. Your *first priority* should be to do the full-court dribbling drills every day, then if you have extra time, do the closet drills.

To repeat what I said in chapter one. For first two weeks of practice be willing to help and allow your players to develop these skills correctly. The first two weeks may be terrible to watch and frustrating for your players. After four weeks you will not believe the difference!

PASSING

To be a good passer you have to realize that one guy's open so you try to pass him the ball the best possible way. Whether it's behind your back, a flick of the wrist, over the head pass or whatever, try to have a vision of the whole court.

Nate "Tiny" Archibald

—N.B.A. Assist leader 1972-73
—N.B.A. All-Star Team
—N.B.A. Scoring Champion 1972-73
—Boston Celtics 1981 World Champions

3
PASSING

In this chapter you can learn:

- •Unselfish basketball passing
- •A repertoire of passing techniques
- •Basic and advanced passing skills
    Four key passing techniques
    Five advanced drills to help your peripheral vision
    Passing drills for team practice

==

One of the most enjoyable things to watch in a basketball game is passing. Nothing "picks up" a crowd faster than a basket made possible by an exceptional pass. It gives the team an emotional lift and breeds a spirit of unity and teamwork. That's why I always say, *A good pass is worth 4 points!* Two scored by the converted basket and the two "invisible points," the momentum gives to the fans and your teammates.

When I think of great passers, I think of players like Bob Cousy, "Pistol" Pete Maravich, Nate "Tiny" Archibald, Earvin "Magic" Johnson, Isaiah Thomas and Larry Bird. These players have developed the abilities necessary to be a good passer:

(1)   They are able to visualize the *whole* court and all that is happening;

(2)   They have developed through practice, a repertoire of

passes they can use for many different situations.

There are some passes which are more difficult to throw than others. A "behind the back" or "no-look" pass will obviously be more difficult than a simple chest pass. But they may also be more appropriate in certain game situations. Basic arithmetic is less difficult than geometry, but both can be effective and useful if *mastered*. Passing the basketball is the same; both simple and difficult passes can be effective and useful if mastered. You're not a "hot dog" or "showoff" if you have mastered a skill and do it correctly in the right game situation. "Showing-off" is trying to do something you have not mastered.

Basketball is a team-oriented game. By developing your skills as a passer, you will improve your chances to show individual creativity and talent. Passing is an easy skill to practice with a friend or alone, all you need is a wall! Practicing drills only a few minutes *each day*, you will have added another skill to your overall game. (*Note: a word of caution. Before you try to develop difficult passes, make sure you have *mastered* the basic passes first. Basketball is a game of fundamentals.)

PASSING DRILLS

I have divided passing drills into two categories: *Basic passes* and *Advanced passes* which are more difficult. When practicing your passing drills pick a target on the wall about 5 feet high to represent the "chest" of a teammate. You can use tape or paint a big "X" or "O" about the size of the basketball on the wall. Remember, *the only good pass is a completed pass.* Good intentions do not help to score baskets, good passes do.

A good pass (except high "lob" passes) should always be received in the chest area of a player. Your teammate should not have to lean over sideways or backward to receive your pass, especially if he is moving.

Begin first by practicing *Basic passes* from 10 feet. Then as you develop and your passes become stronger, practice from 20 and then 30 feet. All your passes should be "sharp" and quick. Once you can hit your target from 30 feet every time, with all the *Basic passes*, then you are ready to move on to the

Advanced passes. Practice the advanced passes the same way. Begin practicing from 10 feet away and practice until you can do them all effectively and without ever missing the target from 30 feet. A good idea is to spend a *minimum of 1-2 weeks* at each distance before moving on to the next one. Do this for both the basic and advanced passes. In only 12 weeks you will have developed your passing ability and gained a large repertoire of passes! (*Note: if you need to take 2 to 4 weeks to perfect your passes from each distance, then do it. Anything worth doing is worth doing right. Do not move to a farther distance away from your target until you have mastered the distance you are at. A greater distance and more difficult passes take a little more time to perfect.)

BASIC PASSES

For all basic passes, you must do three things:
(1) Keep your eyes on the target.
(2) Take a small step forward in the direction of the pass.
(3) Make sure your *fingertips* are the last to touch the ball. (Do *not* let the ball touch the palms of your hands.)

A.   TWO-HANDED CHEST PASS

Begin with the ball close to your chest, push the ball ahead, "snapping" your wrists so that your hands turn inside out. When you finish the pass the top of your hands should be *facing* each other [Figures 3-1, 3-2].

B.   TWO-HANDED BOUNCE PASS

Use the same motion to pass as chest pass, except bounce the ball hard on the floor three-fourths of the way to your target.

[3-1]

[3-2]

92

C. TWO-HANDED OVERHEAD PASS

Good to use for "Lob" passes (page 101), outlet passes for fast-breaks and passes against a zone defense [Figure 3-3].

Hold the ball with both hands over your head. Passing the ball, use your wrist to snap the ball toward the target. The top of your hands should end up facing each other.

[3-3]

D. ONE-HANDED SHUFFLE PASS

Good for passing to a teammate cutting by you or to give off as a soft, easy pass when you drive to the basket. To practice, stand sideways to the target with your feet parallel, hold the ball with both hands. "Craddle" the ball with one hand underneath it as you shuffle the ball to your side toward the

93

target [Figures 3-4, 3-5]. Practice with both left and right hands. (*Practice this pass only from *10 and 15 feet*.)

[3-4]

[3-5]

E. BASEBALL PASS

As you begin practicing from *20 feet* practice this pass *in place* of the shuffle pass. Practice it with *both* the left and right hand [Figure 3-6].

[3-6]

ADVANCED PASSES

Advanced passes are more difficult. To perform them correctly, you must be willing to spend more time in practice. Concentrate on using your "peripheral vision," seeing either side of your body without having to turn your head. Each drill requires different abilities and takes time to perfect. Do *not* move farther away from the target until you have mastered each pass from closer distances. These are "reaction passes"; as you practice them, you will begin automatically using them as you react to different game situations.

95

A. BEHIND-THE-BACK PASS

Stand sideways to your target with your feet parallel. Hold the ball with both hands, then make the pass [Figures 3-7, 3-8]. (*Practice with *both* the left and right hand.)

[3-7]

[3-8]

B. BEHIND-THE-BACK BOUNCE PASS

Performed the same way as the behind the back pass *except* as you swing the ball around your back, you bounce it about half way to the target [Figure 3-9].

[3-9]

C. OFF-THE-DRIBBLE PASS

Keep your eyes on the target. Step in the direction you pass. Pass ball off the dribble with one hand [Figure 3-10]. (*Practice using *both* the left and right hand.)

D. "NO-LOOK" OR BLIND PASS

Stand sideways to the target with your feet parallel. Hold the ball with both hands. Take one step backwards so that you are still sideways to the target and your feet are still parallel. (You should now be about three feet behind the target line.)

[3-10]

Move your arms as if you are going to make a two-handed chest pass but place your left hand over the ball and your right hand to the side [Figure 3-11]. Do *not* turn your head to look at the target but use your peripheral vision [Figure 3-12]. Pass the ball sideways to the target with your right hand, snapping your wrist as you do [Figure 3-12]. (*Practice with both the right and left hand.)

[3-11]

[3-12]

E. BEHIND-THE-HEAD PASS

Stand sideways to the target with your feet parallel. Hold the ball with both hands. Take one step forward as you begin to pass. Swing the ball around behind your head, passing it toward the target and snapping your wrist [Figure 3-13]. Do *not* tilt your head forward. (*Practice with both the left and right hand. Only practice this pass from *10 and 15 feet;* at greater distance, replace it with the "lob" pass.)

[3-13]

100

F. "LOB" PASS

(*Begin practicing at *20 feet* and use to replace the behind the head pass.)

Stand facing the target. Hold the ball with both hands. Keep your eyes on the target. Take one step forward as you begin the pass. "Lob" the pass up toward the target, arch the ball while snapping your wrist [Figure 3-14]. (*Note: If you do not have a backboard to pass toward, use the side of a house, building or even a tall ladder!)

[3-14]

101

COACHES CHALK TALK

Passing is a "habit-skill" and once developed is a matter of memory. It does not need to be worked on every day. Most players are not good passers because they have not learned to "look" at the whole court with their head and eyes up. If you have your players practicing dribbling skills (full-court) every day, they will automatically become better passers as they learn in those drills to keep their head and eyes up and so have better vision of the whole court.

Again, the first two weeks of each season should be used with extra time in practice to develop and resharpen players' skills. This is your "preseason preparation period." You only need a maximum of ten minutes a day during this period.

I do not believe in trying to teach a whole team difficult passes ("Advanced passes"). A player must want to learn and develop this skill on his own. The only passing drills to practice as a team are the fundamental passes. I mention three ways this can be done to best help develop your players.

1. **Wall-passing drills.**

Along one of the walls in the gym (or lockerroom), 5 to 10 feet apart on the wall, put up "passing spots" (use tape, paint, marker, etc.). The spots should be about 5 feet high.

Put your players in 5 to 6 lines facing the spots, first 10, then 20, then 30 feet away from the wall for each drill. Use one ball for each line, with preferably two and no more than three players in each line [Figure 3-15]. Practice the basic passing drills. Do each pass 5-10 times, then move back 10 feet. Practice all passes from 10, 20 and 30 feet.

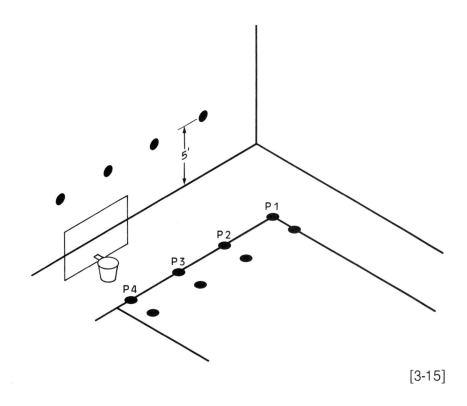

5'

P 1
P 2
P 3
P 4

[3-15]

2. Line-passing drills.

Put 3 to 4 players in one line *facing* 3 to 4 other players. Using one ball, have player 1 pass to player 2 and then move to the right to the end of the opposite line. Player 2 immediately passes to player 3 and follows his pass to the right going to the end of the opposite line, etc. Continue with the same pass until player 6 has made five passes. Practice the *same* pass 10 feet farther apart. Practice all passes at 10, 20 and 30 feet. Passes should be sharp and quick [Figure 3-16].

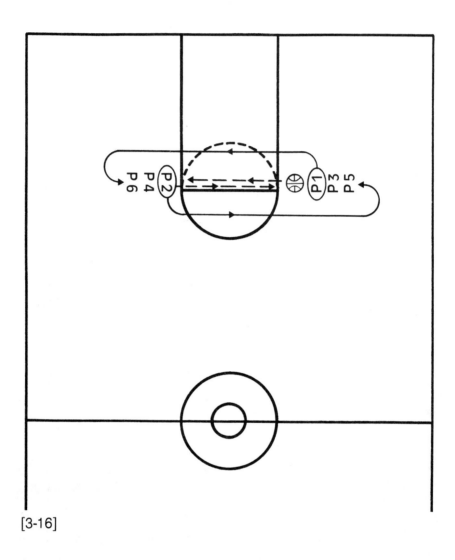

[3-16]

3. Star passing drill.

At center court have the players form 5 lines in a "star" design [Figure 3-17] with 2 to 3 players in each line. Player 1 passes to player 2 and follows his pass to the right, moving to the back of player 2's line. Player 2 passes to player 3 and follows his pass to the right to the back of player 3's line, etc. (*Have your players do the *Basic pass* drills on pages 91-95.)

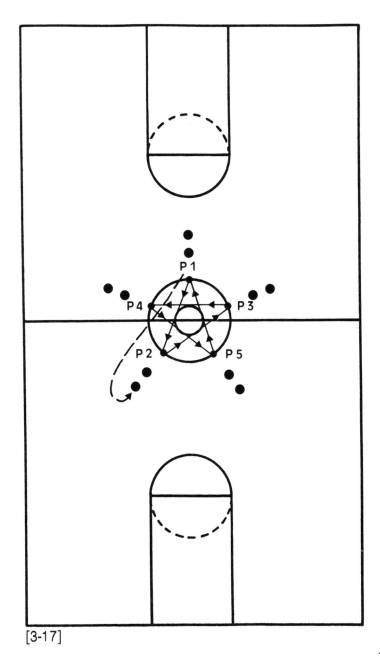

[3-17]

It is better to have your players practice a specific number of passes as indicated in these drills because it will make them concentrate more. They will not feel that they are in a line to toss the ball and use up practice time. Have them work to hit their targets accurately.

A good idea for team practices is to allow a ten-minute slot in each day of practice to work on "habit skills"—passing, cutting, rebounding, working on the "triple threat" of basketball, etc. In this ten-minute slot rotate the habit skills you work on each new day of practice. Your players will stay familiar with each of their skills without getting bored or the drill becoming too monotonous.

DEFENSE

Defender—is one to assert, to guard, to prohibit, to oppose.

Dictionary

Defense is a matter of pride. . . .

Bill Russell

—N.B.A. All-Defensive Team
—World Champion Boston Celtics
1957, '59, '60, '61, '62, '63, '64,
'65, '66, '68, '69
—N.B.A. All-Star Team
—Member Basketball Hall of Fame

The biggest thing about defense is that it's something you can rely on. . . It mostly means being willing to work hard; it's something to rely on night after night, game after game. . . . The thing about defense is that it seems to open up every other part of basketball for you. You start the game and you just drag. But you gut it out, play your "D," and pretty soon you start to get with it. . . . You forget how tired you are and pretty soon basketball is beautiful again.

Walt "Clyde the Glide"
Frazier

—N.B.A. All-Defensive Team
—N.B.A. All-Star Team
—World Champion New York Knicks
1970, 1973

4

DEFENSE

In this chapter you can learn:

- •How playing good defense gets you off the bench and into the game.
- •The value of great defensive skills
  - —8 ways to make defense easier
  - —Ways to disrupt your opponents' rhythm
  - —Man-to-man and zone drills for team practice

═══════════════════════

It is possible to write a whole book on defense. Many have already been written. Since this book is oriented toward helping to develop skills and abilities of the individual player, I suggest ways in which you can improve your defense individually. Before I do that, however, you need to understand the importance of playing good defense.

In a forty-minute game of basketball, approximately twenty minutes of your time will be spent at the defensive end of the court. As you will spend 50 percent of your time playing defense, it is a good idea to develop attitudes and habits to use at this time that will benefit you, your team, and improve your chances of winning games. If you score 30 points in a game and the man you guard scores 25 points, the only thing you have accomplished is to "neutralize" your opponent. However, if you score 25 points and hold an opposing player who is averaging 25 ppg (points per game) to only ten points, you have really accomplished something and benefitted your team as well. If you are not a great scorer and only average 10 ppg, but you hold an opposing player who averages 25 ppg to only ten points, you have made a great contribution and helped your team.

Look at it this way. Your team is the Fairborn Flyers and tonight you play against the Canyon Cougars. You are assigned to defend their top scorer "Sam Shooter" who averages 24 ppg, while you average 10 ppg. Both the Fairborn Flyers and the Canyon Cougars are averaging 80 ppg as a team. When you defend Sam, if you hold him to twelve points in the game, you will cut the team's scoring by 15 percent or twelve points.

Players	P.P.G.	% of team output
YOU	10	12%
Joe	18	22%
Craig	15	19%
Bill	13	16%
Eric	25	31%
	80 ppg	100%

FAIRBORN FLYERS

Players	P.P.G.	% of team output
SAM	24	30%
Mike	11	13%
Sean	16	20%
Greg	14	18%
Ted	15	19%
	80 ppg	100%

CANYON COUGARS

If you hold Sam to 12 points, the final score will be 80 to 68 in favor of your team. If you defend Mike who only gets 11 ppg and hold him to 6 points, you have still cut the opposing team's score by 6 points. The final score of the game would be 80-74 in your team's favor. This illustration helps to show the importance of playing defense and in being a complete player.

It may not be possible to stop a great shooter from scoring completely. You can severely limit his output of points by playing good defense. Remember, most games are lost by *less* than a 10-point margin! Your efforts will make a difference!

It does not take "natural ability," great talent or even being a great athlete to play good defense. It only requires that you work hard and play with your heart. Coach Don Meade always says, "You play defense with three things, you head, your heart and your feet."

PLAYING DEFENSE WITH "YOUR HEAD"

The fact that you want to play defense means you are using your head because you realize its importance in winning games. To use your head in playing defense you need to find the best ways to defend an opposing player or team. I believe for an individual player or team, playing offensive basketball is a matter of "rhythm," habits, offensive plays and patterns, a repertoire of individual shots, moves, and skills they have practiced over and over. Every team has one or two plays that work extremely well for them. All players have their favorite moves and shots they like to make. The objective, then, of good defense, whether for an individual or team, is to disrupt and change the offensive rhythm of their opponent. You only need "to assert" effort and "to prohibit" you offensive opponent from doing what he normally likes to do. Watch him, study him and learn:

— Where does he like to get the ball, in what area?
— Is he right or left-handed, which way does he like to go, on what side of the court, can he use his weak hand?
— What are his two favorite moves or plays?

— Is he a bad dribbler and good outside shooter?
— Is he a good dribbler and bad outside shooter?
— Does he like to cut a lot?
— Does he try to rebound a lot offensively?

These are just a few questions you need to ask yourself as you play defense. Defense is hard work, but it is also good basketball! Use your head.

PLAYING DEFENSE WITH "YOUR HEART"

You do *not* need to be a great athlete or have "natural ability" to be a good defensive player. You only need to have heart. When you have the heart to play defense, it means two things:

1. You have the *desire* to play defense. You *want* to play it well.
2. You are willing to work hard, to exert all your effort.

Anybody can play defense. You do not need to be a great jumper, have speed or quickness or have long arms. You only need the courage to try, to work hard and to play hard. If you want to improve your defense, develop your confidence and conditioning, then make a resolution to cover the best player on the opposing team *every time* you play, whether it is in the playgrounds, gym, team practices or games. It will not be fun or easy at first. Playing defense correctly like any other skill takes time. It must be learned through mistakes and constant practice. Be determined to succeed at being a good defensive player. With time and work you will gain confidence and ability.

Anything out of the ordinary makes a coach take notice. A player working hard on defense *every day*, whether in the school-yards, practice or games can be assured he will gain the attention and respect of his coach and peers. I have seen many players who had little or no talent make a team and develop into good players nly because they had heart, a desire and courage to try. They simply outworked and outhustled all the other players. They played good defense. So accept the challenge, play with heart.

PLAYING DEFENSE WITH "YOUR FEET"

Playing defense with your feet means that you do not "reach in" to try and steal the ball. That is lazy and costly, and often you will be called for a foul. You cannot be leaning forward off balance to reach in and be moving laterally and on balance at the same time. It takes more intelligence and discipline not to reach in. Playing defense with your feet requires that you use the correct steps. Just as a dancer must use the right steps to perform a specific dance, so a defensive players must use choreography in playing defense with his feet. I will define two basic steps and three important tools which are most applicable to the individual player: the shuffle step, the drop step, "pointers," denying the ball and denying the cut.

SHUFFLE STEP

Bend your knees low as you stand on the "balls" of your feet with your feet being a little more than a shoulder-width apart [Figure 4-1]. Your hands should be open with your arms

[4-1]

extended out to the sides to keep you from reaching in and to help deny the passing lanes. As you stay low on the balls of your feet, quickly "shuffle" to your right side *without* letting your heels touch [Figure 4-2]. (Your feet should never get closer than a foot apart. If they do, you will not stay low and balanced.) If you are on a basketball court, stand at the top of the key and go *both* directions three times each as quickly as possible [Figure 4-3]. (*If you do not have a basketball court, use your driveway, sidewalk or lawn.)

[4-2]

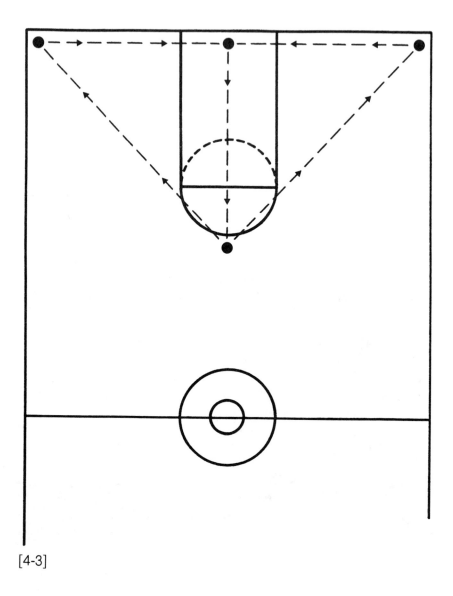

[4-3]

DROP STEP

Begin with your back facing at the baseline in a defensive position. Using the shuffle, step, and staying *low*, move quickly to the top of the key, then change directions by pivoting backwards off your left foot as you "drop" your right foot back behind you to change directions [Figure 4-4]. Shuffle to the half-court sideline and then drop step by pivoting backwards off your right foot to change direction [Figure 4-5]. Do full court up and back two times.

[4-4]

[4-5]

These are excellent defensive drills. You can practice in a gym, on the street, on a sidewalk or a wide hallway. They only take *three minutes a day*! They will build your defensive quickness, stamina and endurance and help you to be in better overall condition for playing basketball.

"POINTERS"

In defensive basketball, your "pointers" are your hands. They should be used for only three things when playing defense: To keep eye contact with both your man and the ball, to deny passing lanes, and to rebound (Chapter 5).

You use your hands as "pointers" to keep eye contact with both the man and the ball by:

(1)   Using your peripheral vision to see both. You should be in between your man and the ball with your head and eyes looking straight ahead. Peripheral vision is the vision you have from the side of your eyes; this is what you use to watch both the ball and the man [Figure 4-6]. If you turn your head to look directly at

[4-6]

the ball, you will lose sight of your man. Where your body is will depend on how many "passes" away the ball is. You take one step backward (toward the baseline) and one step toward the ball (sideways) for each pass the farther away the ball goes from your man. Examples:

1 pass away [Figures 4-7, 4-8]
2 passes away [Figures 4-9, 4-10]

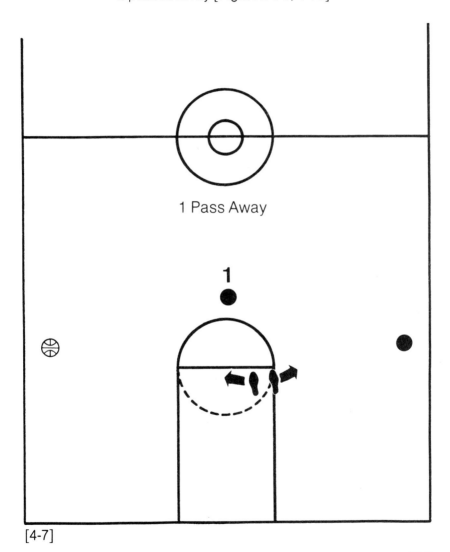

1 Pass Away

[4-7]

(2) One hand points to the man you are defending with your arm fully extended [Figure 4-6].
(3) One hand points where the ball is [Figure 4-6].

By using your hands as "pointers," you will be a better team defensive player. You will know where both the ball and your man is at all times as you "point" and use your peripheral vision. You will also take up space with your arms in the passing lanes and make it more difficult for the offensive team.

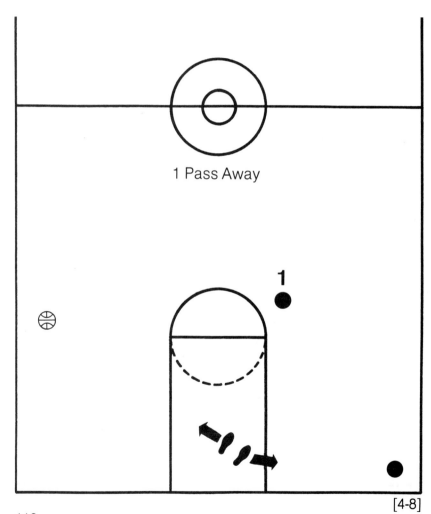

1 Pass Away

[4-8]

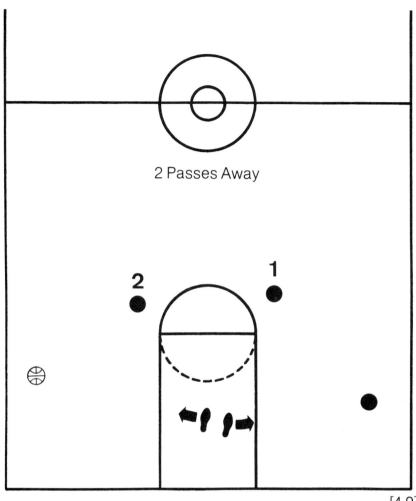

2 Passes Away

[4-9]

DENYING THE BALL AND CUT

"If the other team doesn't have the ball, they cannot score." In basketball it is impossible to keep a team from ever getting the ball, but it is possible to keep a player from getting it. It is possible to allow a team to get the ball in places where they are not comfortable. For our purposes let's redefine this statement. Individual defense: *"If the other player does not*

119

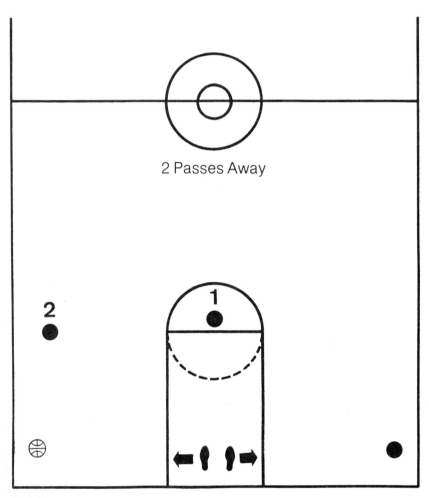

2 Passes Away

[4-10]

have the ball, he cannot score." Team defense: *"If the other team cannot get the ball in a position comfortable to them (that they have practiced), they will have trouble scoring."*

As I was growing up, my father told me to "play the percentages," to do those things that would give me the greatest chance of succeeding. In playing defense individually or as a team, you stop an opponent from scoring when you keep him

120

from getting the ball. If he does get it, let him only get it in places unfamiliar and uncomfortable to him.

All offensive movement in basketball is designed to work in two areas or motions. The first is what I call an "outside cut." This is when a player tries to get open to receive the basketball away from the three-second lane in the perimeter area [Figure 4-11]. The other motion is an "inside cut," when a player tries to get open to receive the ball in the lane area [Figure 4-12]. To play effective defense and disrupt your opponents' "rhythm," you must stop these two motions. Make the offensive player get the ball where he does not want to get it. You do this by using two defensive tools, denying the ball and the cut.

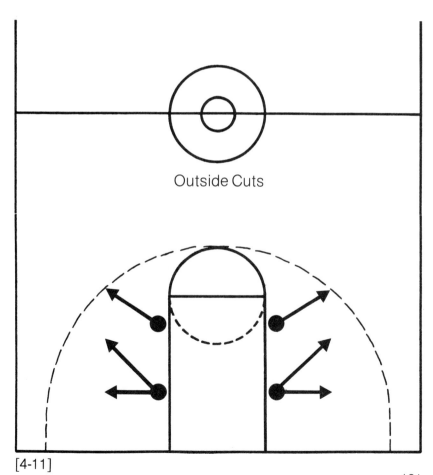

Outside Cuts

[4-11]

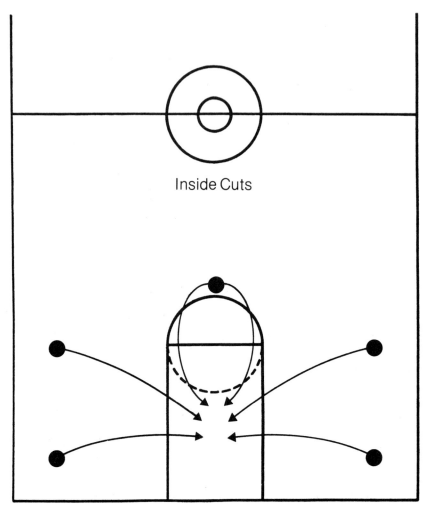

Inside Cuts

[4-12]

Denying the Ball

You deny the ball when your man is within one pass of the ball [Figure 4-13]. To deny the ball:

 (1) Your chest should be facing your opponent's chest.
 (2) Your head should be turned so you can see both the ball and the man (peripheral vision).

122

[4-13]

(3) You should move your feet by using the defensive shuffle step (page 112).

(4) You should be positioned between the player you are guarding and the ball and *be one step closer to the lane area than he is.*

(5) Your outside hand should be in his chest area with your arm fully extended to deny the ball. *You deny the ball with your hand, not your body.* Your body needs to be one step closer to the lane area to protect against a quick "back door cut" to the basket. Players will be hesitant to pass by your hand in front of their passing lane. (*Note: By denying the ball, even if the player you defend does get the ball, you will at least have forced him to get it *outside* of his perimeter area. Then you have taken away one of his options, shooting. Remember, it is a lot easier to defend a player when he does not have the ball, because he must adjust to

123

what you are doing. If you let him get the ball, you must adjust to what he does.)

Denying the Cut

The object of this is to prevent an offensive player from going where he wants to go, needs to go or has been trained to go. You make him go in the direction you want him to go, which should always be away from cutting into the "heart" of the offensive court, the middle of the lane area. Look again at Figure 4-12 inside cuts. Look closely at the shaded area of the three-second lane. This is where you do *not* want your man to enter.

To deny the cut:

(1) Begin by using your "pointers" to see both your man and the ball. (Briefly review Figures 4-6 through 4-12.)

(2) As the player you are guarding begins to make an inside cut into the "heart" of the lane area and toward the ball, step in front of his path with your body, forcing him to go left or right, *not* straight into the lane [Figure 4-14].

[4-14]

(3) Once you have stopped his cut and he moves in another direction, deny the ball [Figure 4-13]. Examples of denying the cut:
—to defend player 1 (P1), allow him to only cut *away* from the ball [Figure 4-15].
—to defend player 2 (P2), allow him to cut only toward the baseline side or above the foul line [Figure 4-16].
—to defend player 3 (P3), allow him to cut only toward the baseline or above the foul line [Figure 4-17].

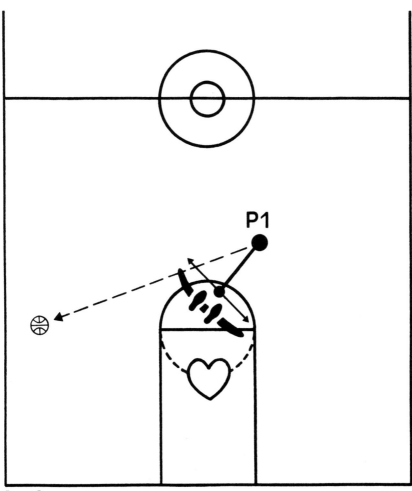

[4-15]

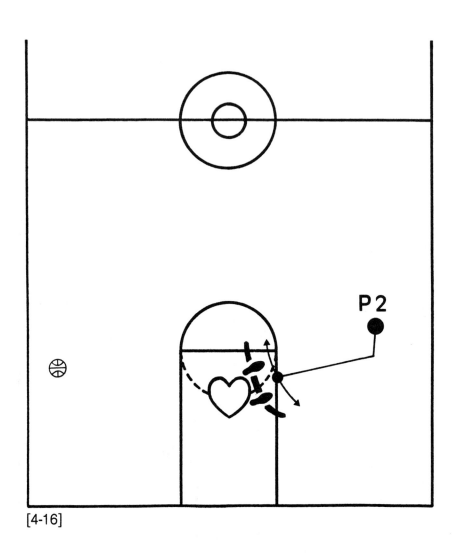

[4-16]

In conclusion, remember, you play defense with your head
(intelligently), your heart (desire), and your feet (choreography).
Your goal should be to disrupt the "rhythm" of your opponent. If
you need a motivation to play defense, consider what you will
get out of it—pride and confidence, better physical conditioning

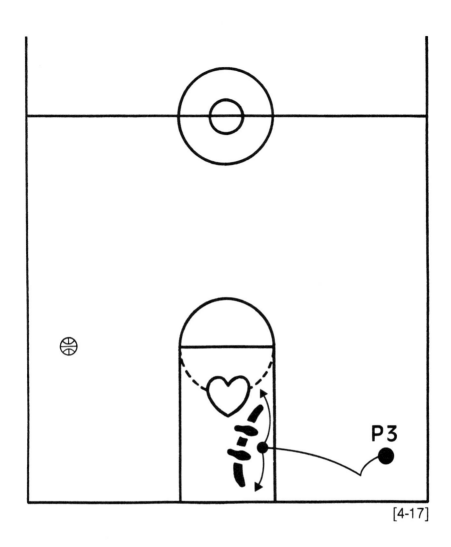

[4-17]

and the respect of your coaches and peers. It will add another dimension to your game and help you to be an all-around player. Most importantly, it will keep you *playing* in games and not sitting on the bench. All players can shoot a basketball; very few can play good defense.

COACHES CHALK TALK

I do not believe that defense is 50 percent of the game and you must use 50 percent of your practice time to work on it. I am not a coach who believes you need only to blow your whistle, look at your clipboard or "shoot the breeze" while the players do some kind of defensive drill.

Defense, like any other skill, requires confidence. Confidence can only come from pracitcing a skill correctly on a daily basis. If your car engine runs on three cylinders, it will not be effective. If your whole team does not practice daily playing defense *correctly*, it will not be effective. An effective coach is an effective teacher. You must pay attention to the details. If your players practice defense, teach them how to do it *correctly*. Teach all of them step by step, and if necessary, in slow motion until they all do it the right way. As they learn to use the correct position, they will, with daily "rehearsals," develop quickness, confidence and desire to play it.

In basketball team defense can be divided into three general areas: presses, zone defenses and man-to-man defense. I will not spend time talking about presses. Not all coaches use them, and there are many different philosophies about them. All coaches at one time or another will use man-to-man and zone defenses. First I will discuss zone defenses, then explain useful drills for both zone and man-to-man defenses.

ZONE DEFENSES

Zone defenses should only be used in two situations: when a team gets in foul trouble, or it is impractical to play man-to-man defense because of the size difference of two opposing teams. I say this because it is more difficult to disrupt a team's offensive "rhythm" playing a zone defense. If you want to use zone defense, however, you should know the three objectives necessary for success:

    (1)   To force a team to throw long, cross-court passes and to take longer low percentage shots.

128

(2) To double-team taller players.
(3) To fill the open spaces in passing lanes and in the middle of the three-second area.

You can accomplish all these objectives in a zone defense by using full extension of your arms and hands to fill passing lanes and a quick shifting movement by your zone defense. Most zone defenses fail to use both of these tools after the first few minutes of a game because they have not been trained. A lot of coaches have our team practice zone defensees and moving into the correct positions, showing us where to go, etc. Then we had no more time in team practice to work on it. We had the knowledge but not the discipline to keep doing it correctly. Most zone defenses break down because of lack of discipline after a few minutes in game situations. Players get tired or lazy and think they can rest because they are in a zone defense. They know the correct way to play a zone defense, but did not practice disciplining themselves to keep working at it every time down court. This "defensive discipline" should be practiced a few minutes each day to develop correct habits. Habit is the greatest discipline of all. Once your players get the habit of playing a zone defense correctly, they will perform in games and play with more confidence and desire because they will see their efforts bring immediate success.

To see the need for discipline, look at Figure [4-18]. This is a zone defense without effective use of arms and hands to fill passing lanes.

Now look at [Figure 4-19] with the same team effectively using extension of their arms and hands to fill passing lanes. This is developed through disciplined practice to develop correct habits. The difference is obvious, as well as the need to train your players to keep their hands up at all times.

The second important tool of a zone defense is quick shiting movements by your zone defense to prevent a player receiving a pass time to shoot effectively and to keep passes out of the lane area.

The best drill is to put five of your players into a zone defense and five players on offense. Put them through a non-stop 60-second drill. Have the offense move the ball, quickly trying to score lay-ups or shots in the three-second area only.

[4-18]

[4-19]

Instruct your defensive players they must (1) keep moving quickly and (2) keep the hands up and fully extend their arms for the entire 60 seconds, working hard. If a defensive player stops doing either of these, time the 60 seconds over again until all do the drill correctly. Have the offensive and defensive players change positions after the drill has been done correctly. Repeat the drill 2 to 3 times for each group. This drill will provide the necessary discipline and develop correct defensive habits. Your players will become better passers against zone defenses. They will also be more united as they work, talk and encourage each other for a common goal, beating the 60-second hand drill!

This is an excellent drill for stamina and conditioning. Once your players develop correct habits by using these two tools in daily practice, they will do them in the games all the time.

MAN-TO-MAN DEFENSIVE DRILLS
(1) *Defensive Shuffle Drills.*
   (A) End-line to the top of the key. Have all your players line up on the baseline of the court facing the sidelines (sideways) in a defensive position. Have them quickly do the shuffle step (pages 112-114) to the top of the key area, then return to the end-line four times [Figure 4-20].
   (B) Triangle drill. Put 3 to 4 players at each corner of the foul line at both ends of the court. Have each line shuffle step quickly to the corner, then to the middle of the court, then back up to the foul line. Repeat three times, then have lines A and B change sides and repeat one more repetition [Figure 4-21].

(2) *Drop Step Drills.*
   (A) End to End. Put your players in no more than four lines on the baseline with their backs to the court in a defensive position. Have them do the drop step drill on pages 114-116. Have each player do it two times, then rotate players until all have done two repetitions of the drill (four times total).

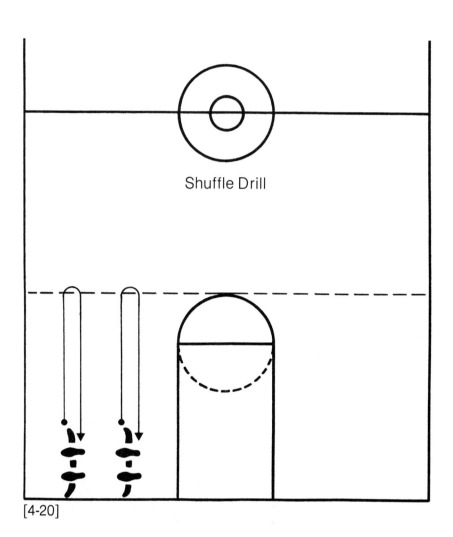

Shuffle Drill

[4-20]

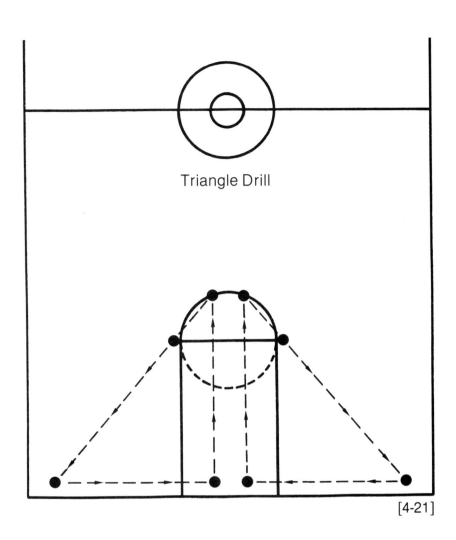

Triangle Drill

[4-21]

(B) Defend the Dribble. Have your players line up in same four lines as the end-to-end drill. The first player in each line will defend the second player in line. Have the second player dribble down the court and back in a "zig-zag" motion with the defensive player using a drop step to change directions in defending the dribbler. Rotate, having the defensive player go to the end of the line. The dribbler becomes the defender,

133

the next player in line becomes the dribbler. Have each player do the drill two times.

(3) *Pointer Drill.*

For this drill do not have your players one pass away from the ball, deny the pass. *This is a three-fourths speed drill;* do it for a two-minute period, then rotate the position of your offensive and defensive players. Place five offensive players in position on the court [Figure 4-22]. Have your five defensive players use their "pointers" (hands) to follow the

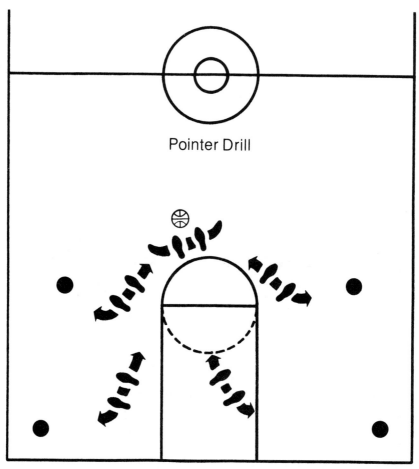

Pointer Drill

[4-22]

ball as it is passed. Unless a defensive player has the ball, he should play one to two steps off his man, depending on where the ball is. Pass the ball to all 'five spots in the perimeter. This is a drill designed to develop your players' peripheral vision, their ability to use their pointers and to learn good defensive help position.

(4) *Denying the Ball.*

Put your players in two lines, one line on each half of the court [Figure 4-23]. You should have a passer (A),

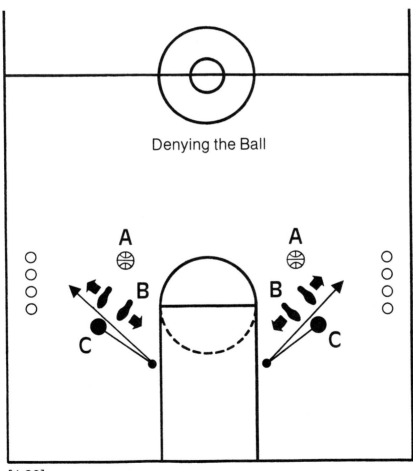

Denying the Ball

[4-23]

defensive player (B), and offensive player (C). Have the offensive player try to get open but cutting only in an angle motion back and forth. Drill is completed after 10 seconds or when the defensive man blocks the pass. If the offensive player receives the pass, do not change places. The emphasis is to complete the drill correctly. After completion, rotate the passer to the end of line, defensive player becomes the passer, offensive player becomes defensive player and next man in line becomes the new offensive player. Continue until each player has done two reptitions of

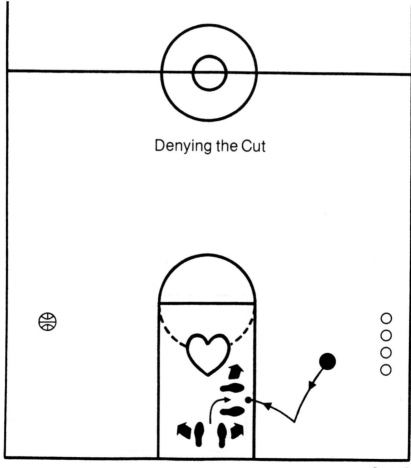

Denying the Cut

[4-24]

all positions at full speed. (*Excellent drill to develop good defensive denial, passing and getting open to receive the ball.)

(5) *Denying the Cut.*

Put your players in two lines at each end of the court. Have the defensive player deny the cut to the "heart" or middle of the lane area with his body, not his arm [Figure 4-24]. Have the offensive player cut up or down as the defensive player continues by denying the ball. Have the defensive player repeat the drill 2 to 3 times correctly without switching, then rotate players. Do at full speed. (*Note: "Back door" passes are now allowed in this drill. The offensive player must try to receive the ball by getting by the defensive player on his cut.)

In conclusion, all of these defensive drills are excellent conditioning tools for building a player's stamina and endurance. However, it will be extremely difficult timewise to practice all the defensive drills every day in team practice. Alternate the drills every other day using half of the drills each time. For example:

Monday
1) Shuffle step and drop step drills
2) "Pointers," zone defense, "60-second hand drills"
3) Team defensive preparation for game

Tuesday
1) Shuffle step and drop step drills
2) Deny the ball and deny the cut drills
3) Team defensive preparation for game

Wednesday
Same as Monday's drills

Thursday
Same as Tuesday's drills

The whole idea is maintaining proper habits; that's why skills must be practiced correctly. Some defensive skills are habit skills ("pointers," using hands in a zone defense, deny the ball, deny the cut) and can be practiced every other day. The defensive skills which involve a lot of movement, choreography and stamina to perform should be practiced daily to develop more quickness, confidence, endurance and proficiency (shuffle step and drop step drills). Both steps are extremely effective when used as part of your conditioning for the team, and you will be accomplishing two things in one. Practice all of these drills the first two weeks every day until they become habit and performed correctly by each of your players. After two weeks begin alternating them every other day.

As you practice these drills correctly in team practice, you will begin to see results in your games. Remember, if you are willing to take the time to be a good teacher, you will also be a good coach. Your players will respect you more as they see themselves improve and become better defensive players because you taught them the right way. Take the time to teach your players right, step by step, each drill in your first two weeks of practice. You will get farther ahead with two "steps" in the right direction than you will with twenty steps in the wrong direction; practice drills *correctly.*

5

THE "TRIPLE-THREAT" OF BASKETBALL
AN OFFENSIVE TOOL

Choreography basically was what I was doing. I had been shown certain moves and just repeated them hundreds of times until they became part of my repertoire.

Bill Bradley

—Rhodes Scholar, Princeton University
—N.B.A. All-Star Team
—World Champion New York Knicks
1969-70, 1972-73

5

THE "TRIPLE-THREAT" OF BASKETBALL
AN OFFENSIVE TOOL

In this chapter you can learn:

- •The Triple-threat—the most valuable offensive skill
- •What the triple-threat options are
  - Drills for the triple-threat
  - How to enhance your offensive productivity
  - Triple-threat concepts in team practice

The "Triple-threat" of basketball is a tool to help players be more productive offensively. It is an easy concept to understand but can be mastered only through constant practice and use in playing situations. Most players never learn to use the triple-threat correctly because they do not practice it. Consequently, their offensive performance as they move up to more competitive levels of basketball improves little if at all, and many players are "pushed out."

The triple-threat has three options: to pass, to shoot, and to drive to the basket. The option you use will depend on the play of the defense. You should always let the defense dictate what option you will use. However, the first requirement for being able to use the triple-threat correctly is to receive the ball within your "perimeter." *Your perimeter is the farthest distance away from the basket you can effectively and consistently shoot the ball.* Converting 35 percent of your shots is neither consistent or

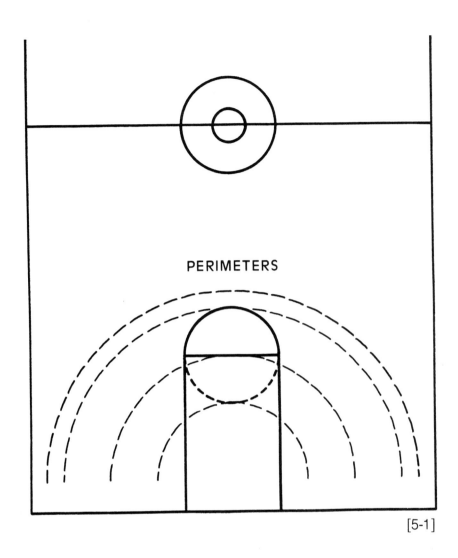

PERIMETERS

[5-1]

effective. A good shooting percentage is to convert 45 percent or more of your shots. Your perimeter should never need to exceed the 20 to 25 foot range [Figure 5-1]. You must decide where you will be most effective and comfortable. If you do not receive the ball within your perimeter range, you have already lost one of your options in the triple-threat—shooting.

The second requirement for being able to use the triple-

[5-2]

threat correctly is to face the basket once you receive the ball in your perimeter area [Figure 5-2]. You should have the ball in a position where you can shoot quickly. Now you are ready to use the triple-threat of basketball correctly.

OPTION 1 — PASS

The first option of the triple-threat is to pass. You should be facing the basket and have vision of the whole court. The objective of the game is to put points in the basket, and since it is easier to score from 8 to 10 feet than from 20 feet, look for cutters and be willing to pass the ball. A leader on the basketball

[5-3]

court is someone who passes, who is willing to play defense, to encourage his teammates and to work hard. Develop your ability to be a leader and better all-around player, be willing to pass the ball.

OPTION 2 — SHOOT

The second option of the triple-threat is to shoot. Once you are in your perimeter area and facing the basket, know where your defensive man is. You have already looked for cutters, none are open. If your defensive man is playing three to four feet away from you, shoot the ball [Figure 5-3]. This should be one of the shots you practice each day (Chapter 1). You should be able to shoot accurately, quickly, and with confidence. If you have made 4 or 5 of your perimeter shots in a row and your defensive opponent decides to cover you closely, this opens up your third option—driving for the basket. (*Note: To practice learning to shoot when a defensive player is playing away from you, put a chair 3 to 4 feet away and pretend it is your defensive opponent.)

OPTION 3 — DRIVE TO THE BASKET

The third option of the triple-threat is to drive to the basket. Your defensive opponent is playing you closely. Look to see if there is an open driving lane to the basket to the left or right side.

[5-4]

[5-5]

If you are a jump shooter, use a quick fake with the ball to the left, holding the ball low [Figure 5-4]. After making your fake, move quickly in the opposite direction as you go toward the basket. Only dribble the ball *once* [Figure 5-6], followed by two steps and a lay-up [Figures 5-7, 5-8]. If you dribble the ball more than once while driving to the basket, it will be easier to stop you.

If you are a set shooter (stationary) and your defense opponent is guarding you closely, jab your left foot (opposite of pivot foot) to the side of the defensive man's foot [Figure 5-5]. If the defensive man does not back away after you jab your foot, then with the same foot continue in a forward direction and begin your drive toward the basket [Figures 5-6, 5-7, 5-8].

145

[5-6]

A good way to practice driving to the basket is to put a chair close to your perimeter area and pretend it is the defensive player. Practice your jab and continue motion or your fake and drive to the opposite side by using one dribble and two steps to the basket to make the lay-up. Make sure you practice going both ways. Practice diving left and right, five times each

[5-7]

day for a month. Driving is a *habit skill*. Once you develop it correctly, you do not need to practice it each day.

The triple-threat is a uniting tool which will help you to get the most out of all the offensive skills you develop. It is an offensive move just like a reverse-pivot dribble or hookshot, yet

[5-8]

is more complex because it is three moves in one. It will fit into the offensive pattern of any coach. It can be an invaluable tool to increase your ability as an offensive player. The triple-threat will take much practice and rehearsal on your part. The triple-threat of basketball is a habit skill. It takes longer to learn. Stick with it and do not get discouraged. Practice each option a few minutes each day for a month.

148

A great drill for developing the second and third option of the triple-threat is to play games of "one-on-one" basketball with a friend or teammate but use two rules to govern the game:

1) When a player is on offense, he must begin from his perimeter area.

2) He is only allowed a shot or straight drive to the basket.

The purpose of these two rules is to help you practice a game situation. Everybody likes to play one-on-one, and everybody plays the same way. They dribble back and forth, back and forth, to get closer to the basket until they get a shot they want to take. In a game you will *never* get the chance to do this. You are only allowed enough time in games for a shot or straight drive to the basket. So if you are going to play one-on-one, do it with the purpose and intent of being able to use it in game situations. Remember, "An exceptional player is simply one point on a five-pointed star."

COACHES CHALK TALK

From a coaching viewpoint, trying to teach an entire team the triple-threat of basketball is impractical. However, this does not mean that it cannot be useful or should not be taught when circumstances permit or necessity dictates. On lesser levels of basketball, for some teams this can be a very beneficial tool if taught in team practices. A lot will depend on the level and individual abilities of your players.

If you want to implement it into your team practices (or to teach an individual player), the best way to practice it is from playing one-on-one with the rules I outlined on page 149. This will give your players live experience at using the triple-threat. The best time to introduce it into a team situation would be at the beginning of the basketball season, in the first two weeks for 10 to 15 minutes a day during your preseason preparation period. Have your players play one-on-one to 12 points. At the end of each week or month take an hour and have a team tournament to break up the monotonous routines of daily practice. At the end of the season have a team one-on-one championship. It will be fun for the players and good practice in using the triple-threat. It is also excellent practice for improving man-to-man defense.

As a coach, I do not condone selfish play on the basketball court. Being a good one-on-one player and being a selfish ballplayer are two different things. As a coach, you go to your best offensive ballplayer for an important basket. Being familiar with the triple-threat and being a good one-on-one player will not make your players selfish. It will help all your team to be better offensive players.

REBOUNDING

If we outrebound the other team, we will win the game; it's that simple.

Kareem Abdul Jabbar

—*N.B.A. Rookie of the Year, 1969-70*
—*N.B.A. Scoring Champion, 1970-71, 1971-72*
—*N.B.A. All-Star Team*
—*N.B.A. M.V.P. six times*
—*World Champion Milwaukee Bucks, 1970-71*
—*World Champion Los Angeles Lakers, 1980, 1982*
—*N.B.A. All-Time Leading Scorer*

6

REBOUNDING

In this chapter you can learn:

- •Rebounding as a defense
- •How to score 6 more points a game
  - Ways to get the winning position
  - Rebounding in game situations
  - How to build defensive productivity

Rebounding, like defense, is simply a matter of hard work. Although being tall or a good jumper is helpful in rebounding, neither are necessary. Both can be neutralized by an intelligent player who is willing to work hard. To rebound intelligently a player must use three steps: have good rebounding position, "box out" and use "leverage."

(1) *Good rebounding position.*

To have a good rebounding position you should be between an opposing player and the basket. If an opposing player is between you and the basket, you have approximately two seconds to get around your opponent to a better rebounding position. To try to jump over someone's back to get rebounds is to pick up needless fouls. Do not be lazy; work to get the best position. You can do this by using two methods:

    (A) *Step and Cut Move* [Figures 6-1, 6-2]. Cut to one side to fake out your opponent, then before he can box you

[6-1]

[6-2]

out, step to the other side to get around in front of him [Figure 6-3]. This works very effectively in offensive rebounding. Moses Malone and Larry Bird use it all the time and are great offensive rebounders.

[6-3]

(B) *Roll move* [Figures 6-4, 6-5]. You can also use a roll
move to get free. If an opposing player has the good
position and has "blocked" you out, instead of trying
to jump over his back or push into him for the
rebound, "roll" by pivoting to one side or the other
and get into better rebounding position. If you are
playing defense, you should already have the most
advantageous rebounding position, unless you forfeit

155

[6-4]

it by not blocking out your opponent. "Boxing out" is the second step to being an intelligent rebounder.

[6-5]

(2) *Boxing Out* [Figures 6-6, 6-7].

To "box out" means to block the opposing player's path to the basket and the rebound once a shot is taken. You may be a great jumper or taller than your opponent and so think you do not need to worry about boxing out. The one time you do not may be an important rebound your opponent gets. That is why it is better to "play the percentages" and use all tools at your disposal. Boxing out is an effective rebounding tool.

157

To box out once a shot is taken, simply make contact with an opposing player by pivoting into him or his path to the basket. Remember, in rebounding you have approximately two seconds to make contact by boxing out and then to turn to find the ball. That is plenty of time to do both.

[6-6]

[6-7]

(3) *Leverage* [Figure 6-7].

The third step to intelligent rebounding is to use "leverage." You do this by getting *low* after you have gotten into a good rebounding position and boxed out. Ideally, you want to be "sitting" on the top of your opponent's knees [Figure 6-8]. This will allow you to:

    (A)   Be able to jump quicker because your legs will already be bent or "cooked" and ready to jump.

    (B)   Keep your opponent from moving around you; you will have "anchored" his center of gravity for movement, his knees.

    (C)   This will prevent you from being pushed away from the rebound position you have worked to obtain.

[6-8]

Even if you are skinny or short, you can compensate by using leverage. The lower you get when you "box out," the harder you will be to move and the more difficult it will be for your opponent to try and jump.

Get a friend or teammate and try boxing out once by standing straight up. Then try boxing out using leverage and being low. See if you can tell the difference.

Extra Rebounding Ideas
(1) Follow the flight of the ball after it has been shot. Four out of five missed shots rebound on the opposite side of the rim they were shot from. This will help you to be in the right

160

place at the right time, and the result will be more rebounds.

(2) If you cannot pull the ball down with both hands, tap it to an area where you can use one of your arms fully extended. This is a very effective rebounding tool.

(3) Rebounding is a difficult skill to practice alone but not impossible. Put the correct rebounding methods into your "mental preparation" sheet and read it through at night before you go to bed, picturing yourself doing it correctly.

(4) If you are a guard or smaller player, you can still improve your rebounding. Once a shot is taken, always go to the top of the three-second lane area just below the foul line. This is known as the "garbage pit" of rebounds because long rebounds always end up in this area. (*Note: One of the greatest games in NCAA basketball history was played between UCLA and University of Houston in the Houston Astrodome. Lew Alcinder (Kareem Abdul Jabbar), 7'3" of UCLA, and Elvin Hayes, 6'9" of Houston, both centers (and later all-star NBA players) were the top attractions. The leading rebounder in the game was a 6'2" guard with eleven rebounds. He got them in the "garbage pit"!)

COACHES CHALK TALK

If you want to see some interesting statistics, go back and look at your rebounding statistics (or any other teams') from last season. You will be able to see a close parallel between rebounds and wins. In most, if not all, of the games you won, your team had the most rebounds. The games that were lost you were out-rebounded. Many games are lost simply because players lack fundamental rebounding skills.

Good rebounding does not require talent, only practice. It is a *habit skill* and does not need to be practiced every day. You should practice rebounding skills correctly for the first two weeks of the basketball season and then once or twice a week in your 10-15 minute daily rotation block for *habit skills* mentioned throughout earlier chapters.

A simple drill is to put your players in three lines at one basket [Figure 6-9]. The first man is on defense and must box-out correctly. The second man in line is the offensive player and must use a "cut and step" or "roll move" to try and get the good rebounding position. Have each player "walk" half speed through all three rebounding tools one time to learn the correct steps and movements. Then do it full speed. Take 3-5 shots, then rotate each position in line. Have each player do the drill 3 to 5 times. Make sure they are boxing out correctly and effectively, otherwise you are just "killing" time, valuable time you could be using to teach and develop your players. Remember, *anything practiced incorrectly is not practiced at all.*

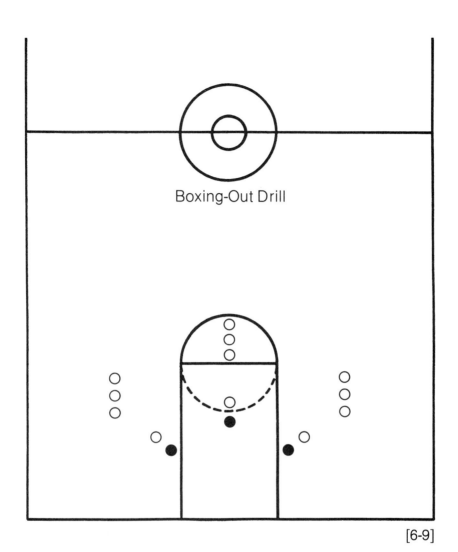

Boxing-Out Drill

[6-9]

CUTTING

It becomes a mental game after awhile . . . you look at the other person . . . you say to yourself, who's going to wear down first? You keep pushing yourself so that you don't give into that game and lose the mental battle. I would see a person get tired and realize, "Man, I got an easy basket . . .

John "Hondo" Havlicek

—*N.B.A. All-Star Team*
—*N.B.A. All-Defensive Team*
—*N.B.A. Playoff M.V.P., 1974*
—*Boston Celtics World Champions*
  1962, '63,   '64, '65, '66, '67, '69,
  '74 and '76

7
THE ART OF CUTTING

In this chapter you can learn:

- •Effective ways to cut
  The better the cut the more you score
  5 drills to develop cutting skills
  Cutting drills in team practice

———————————————————

In order to be a complete offensive player, you must be able to "cut" effectively to open spots on the court if you want to receive the ball. The most difficult player to defend is the player who is always cutting and moving to get open so he can receive the ball in good scoring position. No one can get the basketball by standing in one spot waiting for a teammate to pass it to them. Cutting is the method used in basketball to get open where it is easy to score or to receive the ball in a good location within your "perimeter."

As explained in Chapter 4, there are two types of offensive motions, inside cuts and outside cuts. (Take a moment to review pages 122-123 and [Figures 4-12, 4-13]). The objective of cutting whether to the inside or outside of the lane is to get the ball in an advantageous position. In basketball, intelligence means to accomplish your purpose the best way possible, while expending the least amount of energy and effort. The five cuts explained in this chapter will allow you to do this.

(1) **Step and Cut.**

Step, faking in the opposite dirction you want to go to lure the defensive man away [Figure 7-1]. Quickly "push off" the leg you faked with and step around the defensive man with your hands up ready to receive the ball [Figure 7-2]. (*Note: For all cuts, the most important thing is to "plant" the foot you fake with firmly so you can use it to "push off" quickly and get open.)

[7-1]

166

[7-2]

(2) Pivot Cut.

The pivot cut is an inside cut. Step toward the middle of your defensive man, planting your foot [Figure 7-3]. Quickly "pivot" or roll off your foot around the defensive player into the lane area [Figure 7-4]. As you enter the lane area after you pivot, have a hand up ready to receive the ball [Figure 7-5].

[7-3]

[7-4]

168

[7-5]

(3) **Body Cut.**

The body cut is an outside cut to get free in the perimeter area. Step with your foot in between the legs of the defensive man with your arms up in the air. Now leaning into the defensive man as you step toward him to make him back away, *plant* the foot you stepped with [Figure 7-6]. Quickly cut out to the perimeter area to receive the ball.

(*This cut is extremely effective because it allows you to begin *in close* to the lane area and conserve effort and energy. You simply step into your man making him move away then cut out to receive the pass! Make sure you keep your hands *up* in the air. It will keep you from pushing off, getting a needless foul and keep the referee from being suspicious.)

[7-6]

(4) "V" Cut.

Beginning outside, move 2 to 3 steps toward the bottom of the lane area. Plant your outside foot pushing off it quickly as you cut outside to receive the ball in your perimeter area. The "V" cut can be used to get open in the low-post area also [Figure 7-7].

(5) Back-door Cut.

This cut begins by stepping to the outside if your defensive man is over-playing you or denying the ball. Plant your outside foot, then *quickly* step toward the inside before the defensive man has a chance to adjust [Figure 7-8].

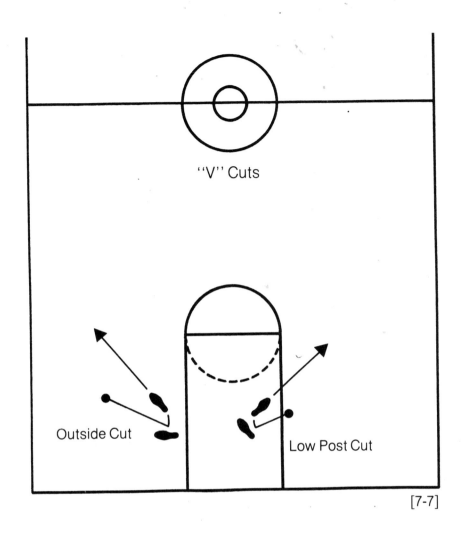

"V" Cuts

Outside Cut

Low Post Cut

[7-7]

You can learn to do these basic cuts without a ball, basket or gym. You can practice them anywhere to be a more effective and productive offensive player. Practice each cut 5 times a day for a month, then you will have developed the ability to be an effective cutter and will not need to practice this skill regularly. You will be able to do it from memory, like your other "habit skills." The important thing is to learn to do it correctly so start slowly, overemphasizing planting your foot and pushing off to move quickly the first week you practice them.

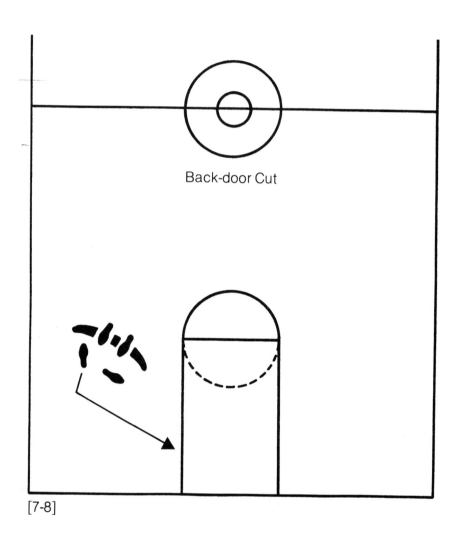

Back-door Cut

[7-8]

The great thing about being an effective offensive cutter is that it will give you more opportunities to handle the basketball. You will be open more and your teammates will pass to you. If you cannot get open to receive the ball, you cannot score points and that is the whole objective of the game.

COACHES CHALK TALK

In implementing these cuts into a team practice, it will only be necessary to teach 3 of the 5 basic cuts illustrated in this chapter. I demonstrated different cuts for both inside and outside cuts. You can decide which best suits your own thinking and needs. You may want to use all four cuts along with practicing the back-door cut.

A simple way to have your team practice these cuts is to put your players into two lines, one each half of the court [Figure 7-9]. Have them practice each cut, doing it *correctly* three

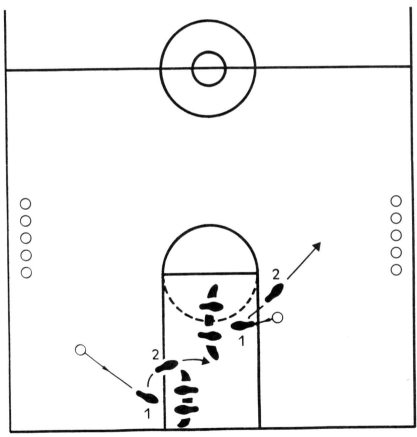

times. Then practice a different cut until you have practiced them all (at least one inside cut, one outside cut, and the back-door cut).

Cutting is another *habit skill*. You can rotate it with the other habit skills mentioned in earlier chapters using a different one for each day of practice. As your players become more proficient at cutting, they will also become more aware and intelligent offensive players.

(THE LAST "TIME OUT")
FINAL THOUGHTS FOR COACHES

At the end of each chapter, I have taken time to explain ways to implement the skills taught into a team practice and defined their importance. I have tried to stress to coaches the importance of teaching these skills *correctly,* the importance of practicing all the *habit skills* (passing, rebounding, triple-threat, cutting and some defensive skills as well) *every day* during the first two weeks of practice. I have stressed that the first two weeks of the basketball season should be used as a "preseason preparation period" in which correct skills are taught to new players and the old players relearn important skills.

After this two-week preparation period, you should rotate a different *habit skill* each day of practice, leaving a 10 to 15 minute block of time open in your daily practice schedule for this purpose. This will allow your players to "stay sharp" in the skills they have learned in the first two weeks without their training getting monotonous or their abilities decaying from lack of practice.

I have emphasized the importance of walking your players through the motions of each habit skill the first two days, so they all learn the correct movements and choregraphy. *You* must make sure they learn correctly if they are to perform correctly. For the third and fourth days, have them do the drills at three-fourths speed, then after that at full speed. Their effectiveness and performance will improve greatly as will their confidence. You learn to walk before you can run, and the same principle applies. Remember, it is better to do a few things correctly all the time than to do many things half right some of the time. You should not expect players to run offensive patterns effectively or defensive presses if they do not have the correct choreography, skills and confidence in their fundamental skills. Correct fundamental skills are the foundation upon which you build a good basketball team.

I have stressed all of these things because I believe it is only possible to be proficient at a skill which is "second nature" to you. A skill which has been practiced correctly over and over until it is done automatically, as a habit, without having to be thought about. Basketball is a game of seconds. If a player has to take a second to think what to do instead of out of habit, reacting to a situation, the opportunity will be lost. That is why making these basic skills a habit is so important.

I leave you with a thought about wisdom by Hyrum Smith, one of the great coaches in my life: *"Wisdom is knowledge rightly applied."*

Use your wisdom and experience and apply it the right way by teaching your players correctly. Very few games are ever won because a coach used the perfect strategy in the last seconds of the game. Ninety percent of coaching is done in practice, not in games. So give "preseason preparation" and *"habit skills"* a try and remember, "When there is nothing to lose by trying, but a great deal to gain if successful, by all means try."

DEVELOPING A PERSONAL TRAINING PROGRAM

Success can only come to you as an individual from self-satisfaction in knowing that *you* gave everything to become the *best* that you are capable of becoming. Perfection is hard, but it *must* be the goal. Others may have more ability than you, they may be larger, faster, quicker, better jumpers, better shooters, but *no one* should be your superior in respect to team spirit, loyalty, *enthusiasm*, cooperation, *determination, fight, effort* and *character.* Make this your motto—your goal.

Coach John Wooden

—UCLA
—10 NCAA championships

8
DEVELOPING A PERSONAL TRAINING PROGRAM

In this chapter you can learn:

- •"What" to practice on your own
- •How to master the fundamentals
- •Personal training, the key to success
  How to build your individual training program

———————————

The difference between being an average player and a good player is time spent in practicing in the "off-season." (It is not difficult to practice when you are playing with a team every day.)

The difference between being a good player and a great player is "how" you spend time practicing during the "off-season."

As mentioned in Chapter 1, "Quality time is more important than quantity time." Anybody can go spend 3 or 4 hours a day in a gym playing, but they will only develop confidence and experience in playing; they will not improve their skills. If you spend all your time practicing and never playing, you will be extremely proficient at doing drills, but you will not have confidence, experience, or knowledge using your skills in playing situations. The most effective "wheel" is well-rounded.

To be a well-rounded player, you will want to divide your training into three general areas:

(1) Development of skills.
(2) Playing basketball.
(3) Physical conditioning.

(3) **Development of Skills.**

It takes very little discipline and effort to go to the gym to play with your friends. It takes discipline and effort to practice alone each day, doing specific drills to improve your playing abilities. Two thoughts on self-discipline should convey the motivation you need to get yourself to practice:

> Heights by great men reached and kept,
> were not obtained by sudden flight,
> But they while their companions slept,
> toiled on and upward in the night.
>
> —Longfellow

> *Character*—the ability to carry out a decision after the emotion of making that decision has passed.

What you practice will depend upon your personal needs and desires. Try to develop your weaknesses and to improve upon your strength. Work hard for 2 or 3 months on 1 or 2 of the "habit skills" you practice. Then change and work on different skills. Do not over-work yourself; it can be as bad as not working enough. You can get tired, discouraged or bored from over-working in a short period of time. You only need to spend one or two hours in daily individual practice to develop your skills.

> Maintaining consistency in the pursuit of one's goals is more important than going after a goal full out.
>
> —Curt Brinkman

(2) **Playing Basketball.**

Obviously you will need to spend time playing basketball if you are to develop your skills and gain playing experience. Be careful that you do not develop bad habits by "overplaying." By overplaying I mean two things. First, you should not play against

178

those who are way below your ability and level of competition. This will only make you lazy. You will not play hard or seriously. Second, play hard for one, two or three hours or until you get tired. If you continue to play after you are tired, you will begin walking a lot, not playing defense and getting lazy. All are bad habits which will carry over to when you play in games.

Make sure you play against the best competition you can find. Try to always practice against players better than yourself. This will help you to develop more rapidly and give you more confidence when you compete against players at your own age level.

Play one-on-one against the best players you can find. Challenge them all but make sure you use the rules for one-on-one give on page 149. Do not worry whether they use the rules or not. *You* use them. It is what you will have to use in games, so practice correctly. You will not always win, do not get discouraged. I played one-on-one almost every day against my older brother and his best friend for over two years when I was 13 to 15 years old, and I never won a single game! After that they never beat me. *Keep trying!* The important thing is not that you win but that you improve. Learn, practice, try harder and improve more, then you will begin winning one-on-one and team basketball.

(3) **Physical Conditioning.**

If you are practicing drills each day individually and playing, you will be accomplishing physical conditioning as you do. If you are extra thin, weak, overweight, have a below-average jumping ability or are a little bit slow, and you want to improve your problem? This is when you should use physical conditioning as an important part of your off-season daily training program, to develop a week area you want to improve on within yourself.

This is the third area of importance in becoming a complete all-around player. Diagnose your strengths and weaknesses then work to make your weaknesses strengths.

The final step you should take in preparing a personal training program is to use a daily checklist of the drills you want to do, for the skills and areas you want to develop [Figure 8-1]. You should not change the habit skills you practice until you have done them a minimum of one month.

Make sure you always practice your shooting drills. This checklist will keep you on target and help you to chart your personal progress and improvement. Just use a ruler and pen to make identical copies of the one shown, using your own choice of drills. Hang your checklist up by your door, bed, on the refrigerator, wherever you must look at it each day. Use it to keep track.

"A goal not written is only a wish."

DAILY GOAL CHECKLIST

MONTH-YEAR	1	2	3	4	5	6	7	8	9	10	11	12	13	14	15	16	17	18	19	20	21	22	23	24	25	26	27	28	29	30	31
Shooting drills																															
Dribbling drills																															
Cutting drills																															
Physical Conditioning —Lift Weights																															
Play ball																															

[8-1]

A "WORD OF WISDOM" ABOUT HEALTH

9
A "WORD OF WISDOM" ABOUT HEALTH

To get from one destination to the next, everyone must use some means of travel: a car, plane, bus, bike, walking, etc. If you have a destination you want to reach in basketball, you need to use a vehicle—your body. Like any other vehicle, your body must be "tuned up" regularly, treated with care and consume the right fuels if you are to obtain its *maximum* use and productivity.

You can keep your body "tuned-up" by practicing your drills regularly and playing. You treat your body with care by not pushing it too hard. Do not overwork it. Do not stay out late every night. Dress properly in bad weather. Do not sleep in every day. Use proper habits in your personal hygiene daily. These will all help you to get more use out of your body.

Finally, consume the right fuels by eating healthy foods and having a proper diet. Do not consume products which will impair your ability to play, function, and think clearly now or in the future, cigarettes, beer, alcohol, marijuana, or drugs of any kind. If you are serious about wanting to play basketball and believe it's "okay" to use any of these negative "fuels," you *are not* serious about playing basketball.

The mental or physical edge you sacrifice will be the thing that beats you. As I have said before, basketball is a game of seconds and inches. If you are sacrificing the care of your body by using any of these things, you are losing a split second of quickness and thinking ability, an inch or two off speed and endurance. You may be able to get by now, but in time, as competition improves and you play at higher levels, those little inches can and will add up. You may miss your opportunity to make your school team, get an important basketball scholarship or a try-out for a professional team somewhere.

I am not a health food addict. What I am, though, is an "addict of life." I have watched many friends and teammates who thought they could "steal" a few seconds or inches off their game and still come out ahead. It has only taken a few years to see how they failed. One is an alcoholic, four never finished college, two that did finish have not found paying jobs. They were all better athletes and more talented than I was. I went farther in basketball because I took care of my body at all times, and I kept trying. Do not sacrifice your chances and opportunity for a few minutes of useless pleasures which add nothing positive to your life.

William Shakespeare put it best when he wrote:

> What win I, if I gain the thing I seek.
> A dream, a breath, a froth of fleeting joy?
> Who buys a minute's mirth to wail a week,
> or sells eternity to get a toy?
> For one sweet grape who would the vine destroy. . .

Before you decide what to do, look ahead by looking back. To predict the future learn from the past by observing the experiences of others. Look at players, friends, classmates, peers, and people who have followed both good and bad roads in dealing with their health and happiness. Weigh the results, then make a decision on what *you* want, not what your peers say is "okay" or "wont' hurt" to do "one time." Nobody intelligent steps out into a two-way street of traffic without first looking both ways for possible problems. This is no different; look at both sides closely. You must plan ahead if you want to get ahead!

10

MOTIVATION

10

MOTIVATION

Napoleon Bonaparte, one of the greatest generals in the history of the world, said: "I see only my goal, the obstacles must give way."

I do not agree with all of Napoleon's political ideas, but I do respect this particular philosophy. If you are serious about wanting to improve, to learn, to become a better basketball player, the only motivation you should need is the goal itself. Things of great value seldom are for free. They take hard work, daily consistency and the persistence of time to overcome all your obstacles. *Obstacles are simply stepping stones on the stairway to your goal.* Do not allow yourself to get side-tracked or discouraged. There is not a successful person in the world who has not had to overcome obstacles. The one day you lose is a day you cannot regain. Only remember and see what your goal is put side-blinders on and let nothing distract you. Practicing your drills each day should become a disciplined habit like brushing your teeth or eating.

"You only have obstacles when you take your mind off your goal."

Throughout this book are over 100 sayings, thoughts or quotes of motivation. Go back, reread and underline all the ones you find. Hang these on your walls to remind you of your goal. If you have quotes of your own that you will like, use them. Take in positive thoughts and ideas, quotes and sayings. I will bet that you know at least 50 negative quotes and sayings that you or your friends say every day. A few examples:

"I'm tired."

"I don't feel like doing it right now."
"It's too hot (or cold!)."
"I can start tomorrow."
"I think I'm a little sick."
"I can do it later."
"I need one more hour of sleep."
"Nobody cares about me."
"It won't hurt to take one more."
"Nobody's watching, it's okay."
"I can skip one assignment or practice."

These are *all* negative, and there are many more! Begin taking in positive thoughts in what you read, think, say and do. Actions really do speak louder than words so take action, "positive" actions.

To help inspire you further, I've compiled some positive sayings and thoughts below. Write them down, then put them up where you can be reminded of your goal each day!

> To every man comes in his lifetime a special moment when he is tapped on the shoulder and offered a very special job, fitting and unique only to his talents. What a shame and a tragedy if that moment finds him unprepared or unqualified for the work (Winston Churchill).

> Blessed are those who dream dreams and are willing to pay the price to make them come true.

> That which we persist in doing becomes easier for us to do; not that the nature of the thing itself has changed, but that our power to do it has increased (Ralph Waldo Emerson).

> With ordinary talent and extraordinary perseverence, all things are attainable (Thomas Buxton).

> The biggest room in the world, is the room for improvement!

Success is to be measured not so much by the position that one has reached in life as by the obstacles he has overcome while trying to succeed (Booker T. Washington).

It's okay to have butterflies, just make sure they fly in formation!

If someone hands you a lemon, make lemonade.

Work is the only fuel the vehicle of success will run on (J.W. Scott).

God doesn't ask about our ability or inability,
but about our availability.
When we prove our dependability,
he will help us with our capability.

(Neal A. Maxwell)

A possibility is a hint from God (Soren Kierkegaard).

A champion doesn't give up, he gets up!

Choose the hard way and tax your talents, God will make you equal to your task (Thomas S. Monson).

The smallest action is better than the greatest intention.

The most valuable gift you give to another is a good example.

Growth is the only evidence of life.

The greatest Oak Tree was once a little nut that stood its ground.

There are 3 kinds of people:
    Those who want to make things happen,
    Those who don't know what happened,
    And those who make things happen.

It's better to shoot for the stars and miss, than aim for the gutter and hit.

There is no chance, no fate, no destiny which can circumvent, hinder or control the firm resolve of a determined soul.

If you perceive a goal, and reach it, you live a dream (Lou Brock).

Make no small plans, for they have no magic to stir mens souls.

Basketball and academics are first and everything else comes after (Julius Erving—"Dr. J").

Each day is like a stitch in your own little pattern. The more time and effort you put into your goals, the stronger your design will be (J.W. Scott).

The only way to coast is by going downhill! (Zig Zigglar).

You can never judge the efficient from the unfortunate, you can only judge the results.

Success is found underneath the alarm clock.

Too many people itch for what they want, but won't scratch for it!

A weak man lets his thoughts control his actions, a strong man makes his actions control his thoughts.

My life is my message (Mahatma Ghandi).

Adversity, temptation, depression and trials come to you when you are doing something right or are about to receive a blessing, calling, or victory. Your failure to persist and keep going will turn them away (J.W. Scott).

. . . guys every year try out for teams . . . but haven't developed their skills enough . . . they get cut . . . you've got to produce now! Coaches can't afford to be patient (Oscar Robertson).

ATTITUDE

11
ATTITUDE

PROMISE YOURSELF

- To be strong so nothing can disturb your peace of mind.

- To make all your friends feel that there is something great within them.

- To look for good in everything and make your optimism come true.

- To think only of the best, to work only for the best, to expect only the best and never to settle for anything short of the best within yourself.

- To be just as enthusiastic about the success of others as you are about your own.

- To forget the mistakes of the past and press on to the greater achievements of the future.

- To give so much time to the improvement of yourself that you have no time to criticize others.

- To wear a cheerful countenance at all times and give every living creature you meet a smile.

- To be too large for worry, too noble for anger, too strong for fear, and too happy to permit the presence of trouble.

—Unknown

As you begin playing basketball and developing your skills, you will develop certain "attitudes." Perhaps you have been playing for a few years and have already adopted attitudes about the game, your conduct and life. These attitudes will be a direct reflection of you and will visible in your actions both on and off the court. Try to develop good attitudes within yourself as you play. If you have bad attitudes, realize that attitude is a mental habit. It can be changed, so change it. It will help your performance as a player but also as a human being. The attitude you carry with you on the basketball court will be the same attitude you carry with you out of the gym and into life.

"Attitude *determines* attitude."
Good attitude = good results
Fair attitude = fair results
Poor attitude = poor results

Attitudes Toward Officials

As a coach I have never allowed my players to talk with or say anything to the officials because I know they do not speak the same language. I know this because whenever a player tries to talk with a referee and the referee cannot understand the player, he makes a funny-looking "T" sign with his hands in the air to indicate he is confused!

In all the times I have seen players talk, cry or complain to referees, *never once* have I seen a foul or violation call changed. The only thing you will ever accomplish is to aggravate an official. Not only that, you will be labeled as a complainer, a poor sport and a "crybaby" by the fans and other officials. Basketball is the only sport in the world where players are constantly complaining to the referees. It is embarrassing to a player, and he looks silly. He embarrasses his team, friends and his family.

I have never known a player who could concentrate and play well while he was complaining to the officials. I have seen hundreds of players stop to complain about a call or walk down the court, leaving their teammates to play defense because they believe they are the only player ever to get fouled or never to make a mistake. Most officials are honest, and they try to be fair. If you do not believe it, watch a game the next time a player complains about a missed foul or bad call by an official. A referee will be so conscious of the mistake he will try and do better the next time. The next time is usually a little later at the other end of the court and to the benefit of the other team!

Referees do not do this intentionally or with malice. Their concentration has been shaken because of a complaining player who embarrassed them, so they try to immediately make up for it by making a "good call." A referee may even become concerned about missing a call, and he may start calling fouls and violations that did not happen just to make sure he does not miss anything. You will cause more problems for the referee and for yourself. He will not be concentrating on the game and neither will you.

I have never seen a player play a perfect game, and I have never seen a referee officiate a game perfectly. However, I have seen players and officials who performed exceptionally well because they concentrated on what they needed to do and tried to do their best.

If you are smart, you will realize referees are not supposed to talk directly to players. (That's why they have a whistle in their mouth!) So do not talk to them. Hand officials the ball politely after a call. It will help you to have a good attitude toward them and help them better to do their job. The result will be a better officiated and played game.

"Good attitudes toward officials create good official attitudes."

Attitudes Toward School

There is nothing wrong with wanting to pursue basketball as far as you can but continue your other interests and ideas for careers as well. Do not put all your eggs in one basket. Give yourself other options and have other hobbies and future plans to rely on. Even a car has a spare tire in case one of the original ones do not make it to its destination.

When I was in high school, I had only two serious goals. I

wanted to play college basketball, and I wanted to get good enough grades so that I could attend any college I wanted. My first year I failed several classes before I got serious about school. I decided that though I had had a poor first year that I would work hard to catch up and get ahead. It did take hard work and two hours of studying each day. I began pride in being a good athlete and a good student and that gave me more confidence when I played. I finished high school, graduating with honors and a 3.5 gpa (B + average). That gave me ''spare'' options to follow if I didn't continue in basketball.

The investment of time and effort I put into studying paid off. I received offers for many basketball scholarships and because I was a good student I was able to choose the college I wanted. My interests in academics had given me more options for basketball as well because I had schools with good basketball programs to choose from. Now I have two college degrees, and they have been as rewarding and important as any of my achievements in basketball in my life.

Don't allow your peers, friends or those you hang out with make you think academics and grades are not important. If you invest two hours a day into school, you will still have a lot of time for your friends and for basketball. Most people waste four to six hours a day doing *nothing* (sitting around, watching T.V., goofing off, riding in a bus or car, etc.). Don't let laziness in school take away your opportunities to play basketball or to have a good career in any field of work in the future. Employers will look at your records to judge your attitude, maturity and effort in the past.

It takes more intelligence to play the game of basketball than any other active sport. Be smart on and off the court, study hard. It will help you to feel better about yourself and allow you to be a positive influence on friends and teammates. It will allow you to have important options in the future. ''If you do not strive to become what you want to be, by default you are becoming what you do *not* want to be.''

Attitudes Toward Teammates and People
The best thought I ever heard for promoting good

sportsmanship in athletics comes from the Bible. "Do unto others as you would have them do unto you." Tensions and pressures can get extremely high, and if you want to "play the percentages" in winning the game of basketball or of life, you must develop the ability to be understanding and encouraging. I have never known a player intentionally make a dumb mistake, a foul or turnover in a game.

You as a friend and as a teammate can do one of two things when these problems occur. (1) You can tell the person how stupid they are and make them feel worse about it or (2) you can encourage them. Help them to concentrate on the game or situation *now*, not the past problem; that cannot be changed.

"It's okay, we will get it back."

"Don't worry about it, let's play defense."

"It's all right, get the next one."

"It's okay, good try."

These are all ways of encouraging and building another. It will help you *both* feel better and work together concentrating on the present and not worrying about the past. You cannot change the past so do not spend time condemning it. If you're intelligent, you will build a positive future with positive reinforcement and encouragement. It will make you a better player and your teammates better players as well.

The only way you can look down on others is by stepping on top of them. You will never be able to climb to the top of the hill by stepping on someone else. Not all players on your team will be all-stars. Not all people will be attractive, funny or appealing to you. (You may not appeal to them!) All people have some good qualities. All want to be respected and treated as a human being. People can be made better by belief and the encouragement of another person.

If you do not like being laughed at, do not laught at another.

If you do not like being yelled at, do not yell at another.

If you like to be encouraged, encourage others.

If you like people you admire and respect to acknowledge you, take time to acknowledge others, *all* others, no matter how unimportant or insignificant some feel they may be.

Again, the simple rule, "Do unto others as you would have them do unto you." By being friendly, encouraging and polite to all people no matter who they are, you will win respect and friendship. If you are a basketball player for your school or community team, people will know you and younger kids will watch you. Whether you know it or not, some young child will want to be *exactly* like you. Be your best. Be an example of kindness, encouragement and honesty. You will have a better attitude and gain more happiness out of life. Remember, you cannot build and tear down a building on a lot at the same time, so build. "No matter what your 'lot' in life, build something on it!"

Attitudes Toward Life

If you are able to read this book, you should already realize you are an above-average human being. You have eyes to see, a mind to think, and an education, which means you have the ability to learn.

This should give you a good attitude about yourself. You should have no reason to have a bad attitude. Look at the millions who are blind, lame, deaf, mentally retarded, illiterate or do not have the freedom or opportunity to read and learn.

I believe that you have the tools you need to get anything out of life you want, if it is for a good purpose. You simply need to seek knowledge so you can develop, learn and progress. Nobody was born successful, a "natural athlete" or with a great personality. These are characteristics which can be learned and developed. Instead of spending time thinking you are worthless or not good enough, spend that time trying to learn, to train, practice, develop and improve.

Every action, thought, effort and attitude will have a positive or negative effect on your life. You cannot build negative thoughts and attitudes and expect to produce positive results. It is one of life's simple rules, positive in-positive out, negative in-negative out. You are the master of your own destiny and "destiny is not to be waited for, it is to be achieved."

I know from difficult and painful personal experience that

not all things in basketball or in life will be fair or just. I do believe that whatever happens to us in this life, can grow, gain or learn something from it. Whether it is learning *not* to mistreat other people from how we were treated or gaining experiences which help us to become stronger and better human beings or better players. I have had games where I played horribly and felt I never wanted to play again (fortunately not too many!). As I reviewed a bad game in my mind, I usually learned something that helped me to become a better player. I had to experience some bad things to learn how to do them correctly. Everybody learns from mistakes. That is why *experience is a lesson to be learned and not taught.* This does not mean you can use it as an excuse not to succeed. It does mean that there is always something positive you can gain from any bad experience. Something you learn not to do again because it is incorrect or a characteristic or trait you develop that makes you stronger, wiser, more caring, mature or humble as a human being.

Life will have many disappointments, setbacks and sometimes terrible tragedies that we just do not comprehend. Many will say such things are an "act of God," "God's will" or sometimes because something bad happens a person must have been "wicked" or "bad." Some will even try to say because of a tragic occurrence that "God cannot possibly exist." The truth is God does exist. He does not control yours or my free agency or freedom of choice or your destiny in life. That he has left for you to do. He will guide your steps though, if you ask him. He will help you to learn from mistakes, grow from setbacks and give you support and strength in times of tragedy. I marvel at those who boldly profess their disbelief in God and spend their time trying to prove he does not exist! Whether you believe in God or not, God believes in you. He has given you life to live, so live it; always try your best and be your best. That is success!

When It's Over

There will come a time in every player's career to have to hang up the shoes, put away the ball and find other things of interest in life to pursue. It may be furthering an education, a

198

job, a career, a family, some type of hobby or involvement in an organization.

No matter at what level you have competed (junior high, high school, college or pro) walk away feeling good about the game of basketball and the opportunities it has given you. James Naismith invented the game of basketball to give young people a constructive physical activity and to help keep them off the streets, and out of trouble. More than likely basketball has already helped you. When the time comes for you to stop playing or if you don't progress to the next level of competition, remember the important thing is not what you have lost but rather all that you have gained. You have been a part of a team. You have gained friendships, good health, positive and successful experiences. You have learned the importance of hard work, sacrifice, self-discipline, good sportsmanship, citizenship, and proper mental and physical habits. Most important you have learned that hard work at whatever you do in life will bring you success. You can walk away with positive experiences and maturity that will help you to find success in other areas of your life.

Life will offer many challenges, realize that basketball is simply one step on the stairway of your life that you have to experience. There are many new and exciting experiences and opportunities that await you. Hold your head up to see them. "What lies behind us and what lies before us are tiny matters compared to what lies within us" (Ralph Waldo Emerson).

HOW TO TELL A WINNER

BY Sydney J. Harris

A loser believes in "fate"; a winner believes that we make our fate by what we do or fail to do.

A loser looks for the easy way to do it; a winner knows that "the easy way" and "the hard way" are both meaningless terms—there are only innumerable wrong ways, and one right way, to achieve a goal.

A loser blames "politics" or "favoritism" for his failure; a winner would rather blame himself than others—but he doesn't waste much time with any kind of blame.

A loser feels cheated if he gives more than he gets; a winner feels that he is simply building up credit for the future.

A loser becomes bitter when he's behind, and careless when he's ahead; a winner keeps his equilibrium no matter which position he happens to find himself in.

A loser smoulders with unexpressed resentment at bad treatment; and revenges himself by doing worse; a winner freely expresses resentment at bad treatment, discharges his feelings, and then forgets it.

A loser sometimes tries to imitate a winner, but he takes only temporary winners as his models; a winner knows who is worth learning from, and who is only a sham success.

A loser is afraid to acknowledge his defects; a winner is aware that his defects are part of the same central system as his assets, and while he tries to minimize their effect, he never denies their influence.

A loser prides himself on his "independence" when he is merely being contrary and prides himself on his "teamwork" when he is merely being conformist; a winner knows which decisions are worth an independent stand, and which should be gone along with.

A loser is envious of winners and contemptuous of other losers; a winner judges others only by how well they live up to their own capacities, by some external scale of worldly success, and can have more respect for a capable shoeshine boy than for a crash opportunist.

A loser leans on those stronger than himself, and takes out his frustrations on those weaker than himself; a winner leans on himself, and does not feel imposed upon when he is leaned on.

A loser thinks there are rules for winning and losing; a winner knows that every rule in the book can be broken, except one—be who you are, and become what you were meant to be, which is the only winning game in the world.